HOW TO SPOT A NARCISSIST

DEDICATED TO MY FAVOURITE YOUNGEST CHILD, AKIVA

First published in Great Britain in 2026 by Cassell, an imprint of
Octopus Publishing Group Ltd
Carmelite House
50 Victoria Embankment
London EC4Y 0DZ
www.octopusbooks.co.uk

An Hachette UK Company
www.hachette.co.uk

The authorized representative in the EEA is Hachette Ireland,
8 Castlecourt Centre, Dublin 15, D15 XTP3, Ireland (email: info@hbgi.ie)

Distributed in the US by Hachette Book Group
1290 Avenue of the Americas, 4th and 5th Floors
New York, NY 10104

Distributed in Canada by Canadian Manda Group
664 Annette St., Toronto, Ontario, Canada M6S 2C8

ISBN: 978-1-78840-6284
eISBN: 978-1-78840-629-1

A CIP catalogue record for this book is available from the British Library.

Printed and bound in Dubai.

10 9 8 7 6 5 4 3 2 1

Additional picture credits:
Getty: Bildagentur-online/Universal Images Group via Getty Images 9; iStock: alex-kava 94, Dimitris66 21c, 35, 91, forest_strider 98-99, Irina Nazarova 150, JakeOlimb 21, Kilroy79 44, Liudmila Baskelovich 13 (used throughout), yuoak 35, 96, 187; Shutterstock: Gopal3366 153.

Commissioned by Stephanie Selçuk-Frank
Senior Editor: Alex Stetter
Art Director: Yasia Williams
Designer: Geoff Fennell
Illustrator: Joe McDermott
Picture Research Manager: Jen Veall
Assistant Production Manager: Lisa Pinnell

FSC www.fsc.org MIX Paper | Supporting responsible forestry FSC® C004800

HOW TO SPOT A NARCISSIST

DR SANDI MANN

PSYCHOLOGICAL ANSWERS TO LIFE'S KEY QUESTIONS

CASSELL ILLUSTRATED

CONTENTS

INTRODUCTION

THE SECRETS OF THE HUMAN MIND

Imagine there was a way to uncover all the secrets of the human mind so that you could understand what motivates us, what our needs and values are, what makes us happy and what makes us sad. For millennia, humans have sought to uncover these secrets through research, exploration and philosophizing. We still don't have all the answers, and perhaps we never will, but this book encapsulates some of the latest discoveries into what makes us tick – and how these secrets can help you live your best life.

PSYCHOLOGIES AND PSYCHOLOGISTS

People often think of psychology as some mysterious art that allows us to read people's minds, but it is in fact a science. This means that psychologists use evidence-based research to advance and test theories, and that any conclusions made about the human mind are based on this evidence. Furthermore, psychology is not exclusively concerned with the mind, but also with behaviour. Thus, the best definition of psychology is that it is the science of mind and behaviour.

THE MIND

Scientists generally think of the mind as being the seat of consciousness, encompassing the ability to think, feel, reason, remember, act, perceive and imagine. All of these processes are housed and controlled by the brain. The brain itself is an integral part of the central nervous system and is made up of neurons, neurotransmitters and other tissues whose activities give rise to what we consider to be the mind. The brain can thus be seen as the 'hardware' for the 'software' of the mind.

The mind includes a range of functions such as emotions, thoughts, attitudes and motivations. These are not always easy for a researcher to access, even by asking people directly, so we often need to observe behaviour in order to uncover the mysteries of the mind. Our behaviour, or the things we do, is intimately connected to our thoughts, emotions and attitudes, so any definition of psychology must incorporate both.

There are numerous different fields of psychology – such as sports psychology, forensic/criminal psychology and clinical psychology – and each contributes to our knowledge in different ways.

Psychology is actually somewhat easier to define and explain than the term 'psychologist'. There is no universally agreed-upon definition of how that title is conferred onto someone. In some countries, anyone can call themselves a psychologist, which can lead to confusion for the public, especially when seeking psychological help. However, some psychology titles are legally 'protected', which means only individuals with specific training and credentials can use them – such as licensed or clinical psychologists.

It would not be unreasonable to expect that anyone calling themselves a psychologist does at least have a doctoral degree in psychology, and most of the researchers and experts referred to in this book do so.

The word **psychology** originates in the ancient Greek word for soul, **psyche,** followed by an adaptation of the Greek word **logia,** which refers to the study of a topic.

WILHELM WUNDT

German scientist Wilhelm Wundt (1832–1920) is widely considered to be 'the father of psychology'. While philosophers like Aristotle and Descartes had studied the mind before him, Wundt was the first to apply scientific methods to psychological research. In 1879, he established the world's first psychology laboratory at the University of Leipzig, marking the formal separation of psychology from philosophy and physiology.

HOW THIS BOOK WORKS

How To Spot a Narcissist uncovers the most mind-bending discoveries from decades of psychology research. It divides them into six core sections and presents them in an easy-to-digest way to help you navigate life's challenges.

1. **LOVE AND RELATIONSHIPS** dives into the heart of human experience. From the science of attraction and attachment to what makes relationships last – or fall apart – this section explores the psychological forces that shape our connections.
2. **SUCCESS AND FAILURE** explores how motivation, mindset and emotional regulation define achievement. By understanding how we interpret and respond to both triumphs and setbacks, we can develop strategies to enhance performance, maintain resilience and cultivate a growth-oriented mindset.
3. **SOCIAL MEDIA AND INFLUENCE** looks into topics such as the modern-day obsession with phone scrolling, 'hate-following' and the experience of 'going viral'. It also explores the Baader–Meinhof phenomenon (or 'frequency illusion'), the cognitive bias whereby an individual notices something more often once they are aware of it.

4. **THE DARK SIDE OF THE MIND** delves beneath the surface of human thought and behaviour into a shadowy realm where deception, manipulation and self-sabotage take hold. While we often celebrate the mind's capacity for love, growth and empathy, psychology also explores its darker aspects, from the subtle art of lying to the destructive force of grudges and rivalries. This chapter unpacks the psychological mechanisms behind these behaviours, drawing on research into body language, cognitive biases and personality science.

5. **HAPPINESS AND WELLBEING** explains the psychological foundations and the commercial forces that shape our pursuit of joy. By understanding what drives genuine wellbeing, we can distinguish between fleeting pleasures and lasting fulfilment, ultimately learning how to cultivate a more meaningful and satisfying life.

6. **CURIOUS QUIRKS AND QUESTIONS OF IDENTITY** tries to figure out what makes you *you*, diving into more existential issues such as our values, attitude, morals, politics and beliefs.

Scattered throughout the book are mind-bending paradoxes and puzzles that will help you understand how your own mind works. There's no set order to reading this book – if you wish, jump straight to the sections that intrigue you most. However you explore, get ready to be entertained, educated and fascinated as you unlock the secrets of the mind.

LOVE AND RELATION-SHIPS

1.

ARE YOU SECRETLY BORING?

If there is one social anxiety that plagues many of us, it is the fear that other people might think we are boring. We'd rather be thought of as almost anything else and, in fact, we may invest a good deal of resources to ensure we are sparkling conversationalists, able to capture the attention of others with our charm and charisma. But what if we are not as witty and engaging as we think we are?

On average, 14 per cent of people report being bored at work because of a boring colleague. Psychologist Dr Mihaly Csikszentmihalyi once commented that 'we're all boring at one time or another, although some people are so chronically boring they're held back socially and in their careers'. Nobody wants to be that person. But what makes someone boring?

CATEGORIES OF BORINGNESS

In the 1980s, researchers at Wake Forest University in North Carolina compiled a number of traits and characteristics that make people come across as boring. Their main discovery was that we find people boring when we have to put too much effort into staying engaged in the conversation. It is not simply that they are talking about things that don't interest us, but that they are doing so in a way that makes it hard for us maintain our attention, follow what they are saying or make sense of it all.

The researchers identified various traits that can make it harder for people to keep the attention of the person they are talking to – and thus come across as boring. These include:

Egocentricism:

FOCUSING TOO MUCH ON YOURSELF

We all like to talk about ourselves – after all, it's the topic we know the most about! But boring people see themselves as the centre of every conversation and manage to turn everything back to their own experiences or opinions. When someone else tells an anecdote, they immediately point out how this story reminds them of something that happened to them. They often like to 'better' the original tale by pointing out how that event was nothing compared to what happened to them.

Banality:

TALKING ABOUT THINGS THAT OTHERS FIND UNENGAGING

Boring people may have niche interests that do not appeal to many others, and they may have nothing to add to more mainstream topics of conversation (such as popular TV shows or films, for example). They may talk about their own interests excessively, or about minor events of little interest to others – long, rambling accounts about people unknown to the listener, or lengthy diatribes about specific incidents (like a hospital appointment) that hold no wider appeal.

Emotional tone:

NOT SHOWING ENOUGH EMOTION IN CONVERSATION

Speaking in a flat, monotone manner, without any attempt to convey emotion – either through facial expressions or tone of voice – makes it harder for listeners to attend to your message. They might become distracted by your lack of emotion, or might stop putting in the cognitive effort required to understand a message that is missing emotional nuances. When we have to try hard to concentrate, we are likely to be easily distracted and struggle to focus – we identify this frustrating feeling as boredom.

Seriousness:

BEING TOO SERIOUS AND TAKING THINGS TOO SERIOUSLY

Humour is a vital part of human interaction that helps us bond with each other, keeps us engaged and makes us happy. It is an antidote to boredom, so when someone doesn't banter or joke, or if they misinterpret or squash our own attempts at injecting humour into the conversation, we feel bored.

Distraction:

HAVING A CONVERSATIONAL STYLE THAT IS HARD TO FOLLOW

Some people appear to be unable to tell a story simply and clearly. Instead of going from A to B, they wander around haphazardly, constantly getting side-tracked. Each new thought that pops into their head sets them off on a new tangent, so that they seem to stumble further and further away from the original point. This random jumping from one topic to another leaves the listener struggling to follow their train of thought. And the harder it is for us to follow the conversation, the more likely we are to disengage and become bored.

I gave 105 of my students at the University of Central Lancashire in northern England a list of 'boring' conversational traits based on the Wake Forest research to see which they found the most boring. These are the top ten boring characteristics that they reported:

Top 10 Boring Characteristics		% who rated this as one of the top five boring qualities
1	Telling long, rambling stories that never seem to get to the point	52%
2	Speaking very slowly	49%
3	Not varying their tone of voice	45%
4	Not allowing the other person to input	34%
5	Telling the same stories repeatedly	34%
6	Talking about themselves all the time	30%
7	Complaining all the time	30%
8	Showing little enthusiasm	28%
9	Including lots of irrelevant detail when explaining something	22%
10	Taking everything very seriously	20%

QUIZ: HOW TO TELL IF YOU ARE SECRETLY BORING

Not all of us are self-aware enough to know that we might be guilty of the conversational flaws described on the previous pages, so to find out if you are secretly boring other people, here is a little quiz.

How much do you agree with the following statements? Rate each statement on a scale from 1 to 5, with 1 being 'strongly disagree' and 5 being 'strongly agree'.

	Strongly disagree	Disagree	Neither agree nor disagree	Agree	Strongly agree
Score	**1**	**2**	**3**	**4**	**5**
1 When I tell a story or anecdote, it tends to take me a long time.	☐	☐	☐	☐	☐
2 I tend to bring conversations round to things about myself.	☐	☐	☐	☐	☐
3 I think it is funny and smart to quote from my favourite movies or TV shows.	☐	☐	☐	☐	☐
4 A lot of interesting things have happened to me that I like to share with other people.	☐	☐	☐	☐	☐
5 I am not the sort of person who is always laughing, smiling or joking.	☐	☐	☐	☐	☐
6 I am quite critical, so do tend to point out what is wrong in the world.	☐	☐	☐	☐	☐
7 I like to tell jokes that people tend to groan at – but I know they like them really.	☐	☐	☐	☐	☐
8 Life is a serious business – I don't have much time for frivolity.	☐	☐	☐	☐	☐
9 I am very interested in a small number of topics and tend to talk about these a lot.	☐	☐	☐	☐	☐
10 I have a few good anecdotes that I tend to tell a lot.	☐	☐	☐	☐	☐
11 I prefer to let people speak without bothering them with questions.	☐	☐	☐	☐	☐
12 I don't have many hobbies or interests.	☐	☐	☐	☐	☐

Total score:	

SCORE: 12–24
Hurray – you are not at all boring! You have a wide range of interests, use lots of emotional range in your language, listen to other people and let them talk. You have lots to talk about because you lead an interesting and varied life but you are just as interested in finding out more about other people. While you like to have bit of a moan and gossip sometimes, you don't constantly complain. You manage to tell a story without going off on multiple irrelevant tangents and you speak with enthusiasm about interesting topics that are not all about 'me me me'.

SCORE: 25–36
Your scores suggest that you may be at risk of boring people, but do not fear – there is hope for you yet. Being aware of your potentially boring habits is the first step to changing them. Perhaps you tell long, rambling stories that never seem to get to the point, or you include every single detail because you think your audience will be fascinated (they won't). Or maybe you speak very slowly or tell the same joke or story over and over again. Perhaps you love to talk about yourself. Take note – and make some changes!

SCORE 37–48
You may be a fascinating person, full of interesting tales and life experiences – but sadly, others may find you boring. Perhaps your main interest in life is something rather obscure and niche (to most other people, at least), and you like to talk about this subject incessantly, steering every conversation back to your preferred topic. Perhaps you don't show enough interest in other people and what they have to say, ignoring their attempts to engage in an actual two-way conversation. Life is a serious business for you, so you prefer to avoid small talk or humour. But all these habits can be changed once you are aware of them – if you want to, of course! Broaden your interests so that you have a wider range of topics to talk about, ask people about themselves more and keep your anecdotes brief (and fresh!).

THE PSYCHOLOGY BEHIND 'LOVE AT FIRST SIGHT'

Those who claim to have experienced it say that love at first sight is a beautiful thing: eyes meeting across a crowded room, hearts pounding and boom...cupid's arrow has found its target. But is there any evidence to explain such a phenomenon? Is love at first sight real?

Love is a chemical reaction caused by a heady surge of neurotransmitters and hormones. The main players are:

DOPAMINE:
The 'feel-good' pleasure hormone.

ADRENALIN AND ENDORPHINS:
The chemicals that make us feel excited and primed for action.

OXYTOCIN:
The 'love' hormone, which plays a role in sexual arousal, romantic attachment and bonding.

SEROTONIN:
This decreases, which can make feelings about the relationship intense and all-consuming.

When these chemicals are released, they cause increased blood flow to the brain's 'reward circuit', consisting of the hippocampus, amygdala and limbic system, which all help us feel good. We can interpret that feeling as love and when we first spot a person with whom we may later develop a romantic relationship, in hindsight we say that it was 'love at first sight'.

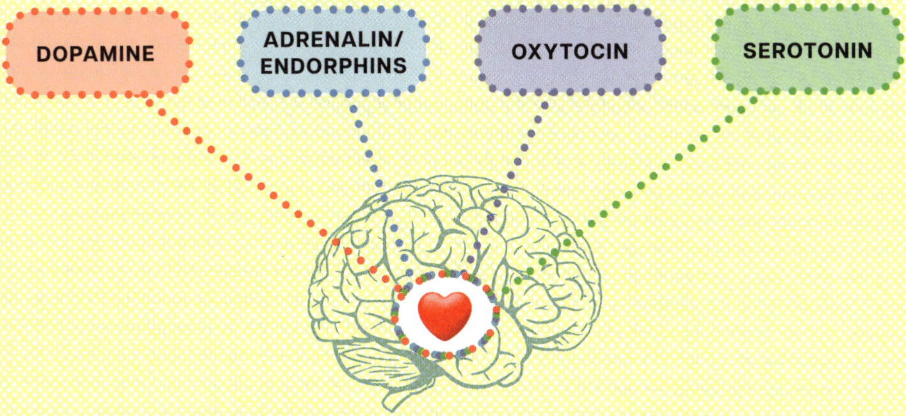

Signs that we may be experiencing love at first sight include:

- Feeling a strong physical attraction to the person.
- Experiencing an intense bond with the other person like there is some connection, even though you hardly know them.
- Experiencing an intense need to be with them and see them again.
- All other concerns and preoccupations melt away – nothing else matters except you and them.

However, statistics suggest that such a powerful event, while theoretically possible, is not all that common. While 60 per cent of people in some surveys claim to have experienced love at first sight, this does not mean that this love became forever love. It is far more likely that they fell into infatuation or even lust at first sight – and the odds of that turning into a forever relationship are small. For a long-term relationship to develop, we need passion, intimacy and commitment. Passion is the 'love at first sight' element but we need the other two to grow that love into a future together.

CAN SCIENCE HELP YOU AVOID A BREAKUP?

Sometimes, couples just need to break up – the relationship has run its course, you are no longer in love or your partnership is toxic. But the application of science can help keep a good relationship from going sour by offering valuable insights into building and maintaining healthy, resilient relationships. By applying principles from psychology and social science, couples can strengthen their bond and navigate challenges more effectively.

Here's how science can help:

1 **STRENGTHEN COMMUNICATION**
Many relationships break down due to poor communication. According to the relationship scientist Dr John Gottman, 94 per cent of divorces can be predicted by the following four communication styles:

- **Criticism:** Constant or over-criticism can hurt and cause feelings of rejection.
- **Contempt:** Mocking or treating a partner with disrespect is a powerful predictor of future relationship breakdown.
- **Defensiveness:** When someone is constantly justifying their actions or making excuses, the other person can feel unheard or invalidated.
- **Stonewalling:** Withdrawal or refusing to engage can be protective and help avoid further conflict, but it is also a serious sign of a failing relationship.

Being aware of these communication styles is the first step to trying to change them. Replacing them with compromise and putting the needs of your partner before your own can help stabilize and grow a relationship that may have been struggling.

2 MANAGE CONFLICT

Conflict is normal within a relationship. Two people, however much in love, are never going to always want the same things, feel the same way or have the same belief system or values. This is when conflict arises, but the science of relationships can help turn negative conflict into positive learning opportunities.

The science of conflict resolution always starts with good communication, of course, but some additional tips include:

- Don't focus on being right or 'winning'.
- Pick your battles – let go of whatever you can let go of and focus on the hard lines, not the small stuff.
- Keep an argument to one specific topic at a time and don't make it about general stuff that you are unhappy with (John Gottman calls this 'kitchen-sinking', where everything but the kitchen sink is thrown into an argument).
- Compromise where possible – and sometimes agree to disagree, too.
- Try to avoid the blame game.
- Avoid key 'hot' words like 'never' (You never help around the house!) and 'always' (You always leave such a mess!).

3 PUT IN THE EFFORT

Love is not enough to keep a couple together – it requires effort. John Gottman uses the second law of thermodynamics as a metaphor for the amount of effort required to keep a relationship alive. This law states that a closed system degenerates over time unless energy is added. Within a relationship this means that even if you don't do anything wrong, the relationship will get worse over time unless you put in effort to improve things. The dynamics of a relationship also dictate that both partners need to put in roughly equal effort, otherwise there is what is known as an 'effort gap'.

That's not to say that it always has to be 50/50, with each person putting in the same effort all the time and in the same ways. Sometimes one partner will be depleted, feeling at a 20 out of 100, for example, and the other will be able to carry the extra effort and be at 80 for them. But there will be days when your partner is at 10 while you're at just 35 yourself. That's when you to need to sit down together and talk about how to get through this time without hurting each other. A partnership can work when you are able to carry each other when needed, and come up with a plan of kindness when you are both feeling low.

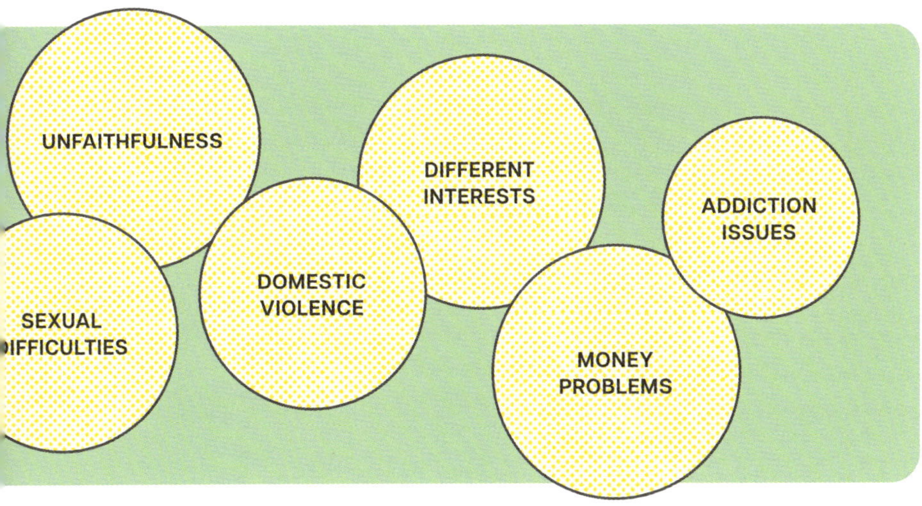

HOW MANY FRIENDS SHOULD I HAVE?

Many people worry that they are not popular or that they don't have 'enough' friends. Social media plays a big part in this perception. In the 'old' days, we would never really have been aware of social events or friendships that we were missing out on. Nowadays, everything is posted on social media, so we are painfully aware if we have not been invited to something or if other people are doing things without us. Everyone, it seems, has more friends than we do. Yet according to a 2021 survey, the average person has between three and five close friends, with almost 50 per cent of people having fewer than three.

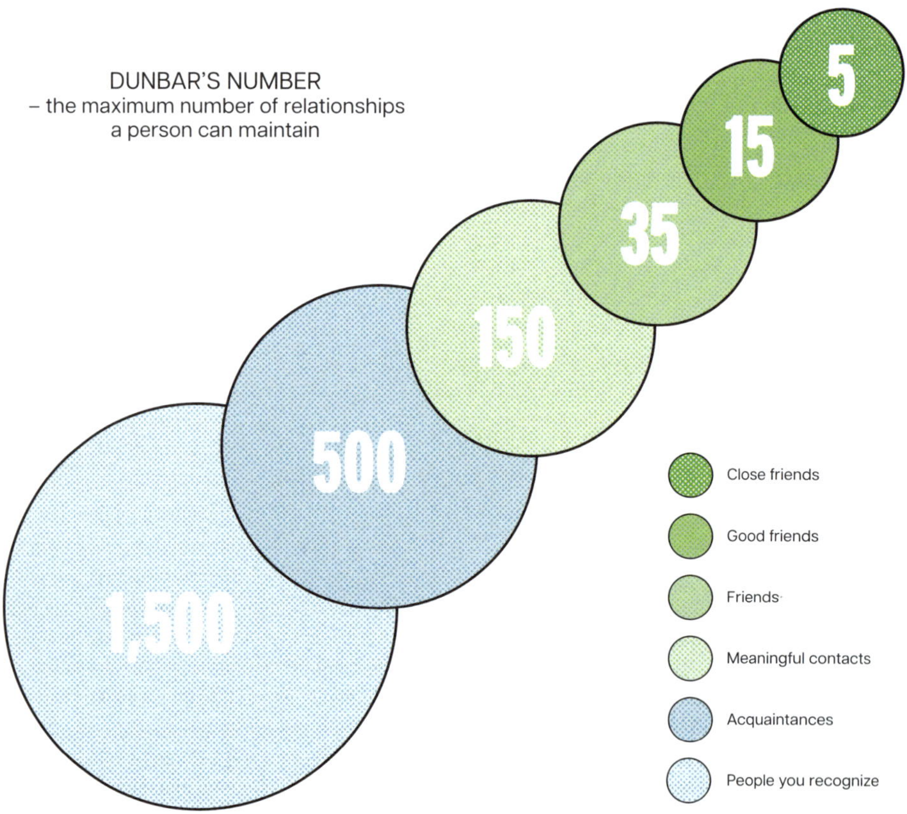

Psychological research has shown us how many friends we should have. This number is known as 'Dunbar's Number' after British anthropologist Robin Dunbar, who came up with this theory in the 1990s. He found that while we may have many acquaintances (around 150, including relatives), we actually only need around five close friends. In fact, humans aren't really able to maintain more close friendships than that. Dunbar studied group sizes in primates relative to brain size and concluded that the relative size of the neocortex – the part of the brain associated with cognition and language – maps directly onto the size of a social group. This ratio limits how much complexity a social brain can cognitively cope with. He concluded that humans don't really have the capacity to maintain more than five close friendships. This is because we humans need to invest time and energy to keep close friendships healthy. According to research conducted by Jeffrey Hall at the University of Kansas in 2018, really close friendships need around 300 hours of input to develop.

DUNBAR'S NUMBER

People can move in and out of each category (which explains why we change friend groups a lot – see page 28) but there needs to be a vacancy before this can happen. So, if you have around five close friends – the kind of people you can confide in – you're doing great. The FOMO you experience when you see all those Instas of people having fun is probably because you're mistaking other people's 'friends' for 'close friends'.

Friends categories	Ideal number	How many do you have?
Close friends	5	
Good friends	15	
Friends	50	
Meaningful contacts	150	
Acquaintances	500	
People you recognize	1,500	

WHY YOUR FRIEND GROUP KEEPS CHANGING (AND HOW TO KEEP IT MORE STABLE)

It is normal for our friendship groups to change over time. Over the course of our lives, we enter different stages and our interests often evolve over time too. According to research in 2021 that examined the social lives of 2,000 people, we lose around 50 per cent of the friendships we make over the years. Only 17 per cent of respondents had the same friends for more than 30 years. Should we be worried that our friend groups are perhaps changing too much? And can the application of psychology reduce the amount of transitioning?

If you feel the issue is that you can never keep friends, it is perhaps worth examining your own attachment styles. Attachment theory was developed by the British psychiatrist John Bowlby (1907–90), who proposed that our early interactions with our caregivers dictate how we continue to relate to other people throughout our lives. The science of attachment styles can help you figure out whether perhaps it's not them, but you.

According to Bowlby's theory, there are four main attachment styles:

1. **SECURE**
   Children with secure attachment styles grew up feeling safe and secure in the love they were given. This means that they feel comfortable and safe to explore new relationships throughout their lives. They trust others and have no problem with intimacy, as well as with the give and take of a healthy relationship. They respect boundaries and can develop comfortable bonds based on mutual respect.

2 **ANXIOUS/PREOCCUPIED**
Children who grow up unsure about the love of their caregivers will later worry about whether others will like them or abandon them. They may be clingy or needy and their self-worth is dependent on social bonds; they need friends to prove that they are worthy. This can make them dependent on others for validation and support, and in need of constant reassurance. They may even get possessive or jealous if their friends spend time with other people and they may spend a lot of time monitoring social media to check if their friends are excluding them. This neediness can lead other people to withdraw from them, which only serves to confirm their fear that people leave them (thereby keeping the cycle going).

3 **AVOIDANT/DISMISSIVE**
Children who are actively ignored or dismissed by their caregivers grow up expecting other people to reject them too. This can make them very independent and they can appear not to need the intimacy of close friends. They keep their emotional distance and their friends may feel that they can never really get close. As a result, their friends may see the relationship as one-sided and start to back away.

4 **DISORGANIZED/FEARFUL-AVOIDANT**
Children who grow up experiencing an erratic pattern of caregiving never know quite how they will be treated. This makes them fearful and insecure about other relationships. They want close friendships, but they also fear them, because they might lead to rejection. This can lead to them 'blowing hot and cold', as they constantly battle between getting close to people and then withdrawing when they feel they are getting too close. Friends may get confused and not know where they stand – and thus back away from the friendship.

Understanding your own attachment style is the first step to trying to change the behaviours that might be leading to too many friendship ruptures.

QUIZ: WHAT IS YOUR ATTACHMENT STYLE?

To find out more about your attachment styles, rate each statement below on a scale from 1 to 5, with 1 being 'strongly disagree' and 5 being 'strongly agree'.

Part 1: Secure Attachment					
	Strongly disagree	Disagree	Neither agree nor disagree	Agree	Strongly agree
Score	**1**	**2**	**3**	**4**	**5**
1 I feel comfortable depending on others and having them depend on me.	☐	☐	☐	☐	☐
2 I find it easy to get close to others in relationships.	☐	☐	☐	☐	☐
3 I trust that my partner (or close friends) cares about me and won't leave.	☐	☐	☐	☐	☐
4 I don't often worry about being abandoned or unloved.	☐	☐	☐	☐	☐
5 I feel secure expressing my feelings and needs in relationships.	☐	☐	☐	☐	☐
Total score:					

Part 2: Anxious/Preoccupied Attachment					
	Strongly disagree	Disagree	Neither agree nor disagree	Agree	Strongly agree
Score	**1**	**2**	**3**	**4**	**5**
1 I often worry that my friends don't like me as much as I like them.	☐	☐	☐	☐	☐
2 I need a lot of reassurance in relationships.	☐	☐	☐	☐	☐
3 I fear that if I don't stay close, my partner (or friends) will lose interest.	☐	☐	☐	☐	☐
4 I find myself overanalysing texts and interactions in my relationships.	☐	☐	☐	☐	☐
5 I feel very anxious when my friends are distant or unavailable.	☐	☐	☐	☐	☐
Total score:					

Part 3: Avoidant/Dismissive Attachment					
	Strongly disagree	Disagree	Neither agree nor disagree	Agree	Strongly agree
Score	**1**	**2**	**3**	**4**	**5**
1 I feel uncomfortable depending on others, even in close relationships.	☐	☐	☐	☐	☐
2 I prefer to be independent rather than relying on others.	☐	☐	☐	☐	☐
3 I find it difficult to trust others fully.	☐	☐	☐	☐	☐
4 I tend to pull away when someone tries to get too close to me.	☐	☐	☐	☐	☐
5 I value my personal space and alone time more than intimacy.	☐	☐	☐	☐	☐
Total score:					

Part 4: Disorganized/Fearful-Avoidant Attachment					
	Strongly disagree	Disagree	Neither agree nor disagree	Agree	Strongly agree
Score	**1**	**2**	**3**	**4**	**5**
1 I want close relationships but feel afraid of being hurt.	☐	☐	☐	☐	☐
2 I sometimes push people away, even when I want connection.	☐	☐	☐	☐	☐
3 I struggle with both trusting and depending on others.	☐	☐	☐	☐	☐
4 I experience conflicting emotions about intimacy – I crave it but fear it.	☐	☐	☐	☐	☐
5 My past relationships have been full of highs and lows, and I struggle to feel stable.	☐	☐	☐	☐	☐
Total score:					

Scores above 20 indicate that you may have that attachment style. It is also possible to have a mix of attachment styles.

HOW TO IMPROVE OR ADAPT YOUR ATTACHMENT STYLE

Now that you know your attachment style, here's how to develop a more secure attachment in your relationships.

Secure Attachment

If you're already secure, you trust other people and feel safe in relationships. You balance independence and intimacy well, you communicate openly and handle conflicts in a healthy way.

How to maintain it:

- Keep practising clear communication about your needs.
- Choose friends who also have a secure attachment style (or are working towards it).
- Be a source of stability for anxious or avoidant friends while setting healthy boundaries.

Anxious/Preoccupied Attachment

If you scored high in anxious attachment you may fear abandonment and crave constant reassurance. You tend to overanalyse other people's actions and you might feel anxious when your friends are distant.

How to improve it:

- Build your self-worth outside of relationships – invest in friendships, hobbies and personal goals.
- Communicate your needs without overwhelming others (for example, 'I sometimes feel insecure when you don't respond quickly. Can we talk about this?').
- Challenge anxious thoughts – just because someone is busy doesn't mean they're pulling away from you.

Avoidant/Dismissive Attachment

If you scored high in avoidant attachment, you might feel uncomfortable depending on others. You tend to withdraw when things get too intimate, and you prioritize independence over emotional connection.

How to improve it:

- Allow yourself to depend on others in small ways and build trust over time.
- Practise sharing feelings, even if it's uncomfortable at first (start small, like expressing when you're happy or sad).
- Challenge the belief that needing someone means losing your independence – secure attachment allows both.

Disorganized/Fearful-Avoidant Attachment

If you scored high in fearful attachment, you crave closeness but also fear it – you push people away even when you want connection. Your past relationships may have been intense or unstable.

How to improve it:

- Identify past trauma that may be affecting your relationships – therapy can help.
- Work on self-trust first – become more aware of your emotions and reactions.
- Take relationships slowly – build trust step by step instead of jumping between closeness and withdrawal.

WHY WE ARE ALWAYS ATTRACTED TO THE WRONG PEOPLE

Do the people you fall in love with always end up being the wrong match – for the same reasons? Perhaps they always turn out to be too controlling or clingy, unfaithful or even downright abusive. Maybe you also find yourself gravitating to a certain type of 'friend' – someone who puts you down, makes you feel bad or just isn't that into you.

If this is you, perhaps you find yourself frustrated that this keeps happening over and over again. But it isn't your fault. There is nothing wrong with you that you keep seeking out unhelpful relationships. It's all to do with psychology.

There are three main psychological reasons why we fall for a type, even when that type does us no favours:

1. **HUMANS WILL ALWAYS CRAVE A FAMILIAR HELL OVER AN UNFAMILIAR HEAVEN**
   This means that we often prefer uncomfortable yet familiar settings to a more pleasant new one. We might not like the uncomfortable one but at least we know where we are with it. We may be hard-wired that way – if something is familiar, that means we have survived it and thus it feels safer. When our nervous system perceives behaviours or patterns that are already deeply ingrained, it perceives these as safe and thus predictable and comfortable. Our nervous system prefers predictability, because it recognizes that this pattern has not caused previous harm. A new or unfamiliar experience thus carries more risk because there are no familiar patterns ingrained in the nervous system to match it against. Something new can thus trigger the nervous system to produce the fight or flight response that is associated with anxiety.

   Often we spend our adulthood searching for relationships that help us to re-create the bonds and patterns that impacted us so powerfully in our early years. This is why people who experienced a lot of conflict at home in childhood might find themselves attracted to partners (and friends) who come with a lot of drama. It also explains why people who are in abusive relationships may find it so hard to leave.

2 WE MAY HAVE LOW SELF-ESTEEM

If we don't think very highly of ourselves then we don't think we deserve to be treated well. This then leads us down a path of being attracted to people who confirm our own self-view, however unhappy that makes us feel. Our low self-worth may also mean we become people pleasers, determined to put other people's needs above our own. This means we can be poor at setting boundaries and the people we care about might take advantage and walk all over us. This may keep happening while we have such a low view of ourselves. See page 36 for more on the hidden signs of low self-esteem.

3 WE MAY HAVE A DYSFUNCTIONAL ATTACHMENT STYLE

Attachment styles are ways of relating to meaningful people in our lives that develop from childhood. The theory of attachment styles was developed in 1973 by John Bowlby who found that if we don't form strong, healthy attachment bonds with our caregivers for whatever reason (perhaps parents were absent a lot, unwell, unavailable, etc.) then we can develop unhealthy, insecure attachment styles that can make us over-anxious in relationships. (See page 28 for more on attachment styles). Researchers have identified certain triggers in relationships that can evoke anxiety and insecurity in people with these unhealthy attachment styles; these include any signs of rejection, conflict or arguments, lack of availability and lack of reassurance. When triggered, this can mean we behave in certain ways that make other people uncomfortable. For example, we may become very needy, which can cause the people we care about to distance themselves from us. We then wonder why all the people we fall for drop us or seem uninterested.

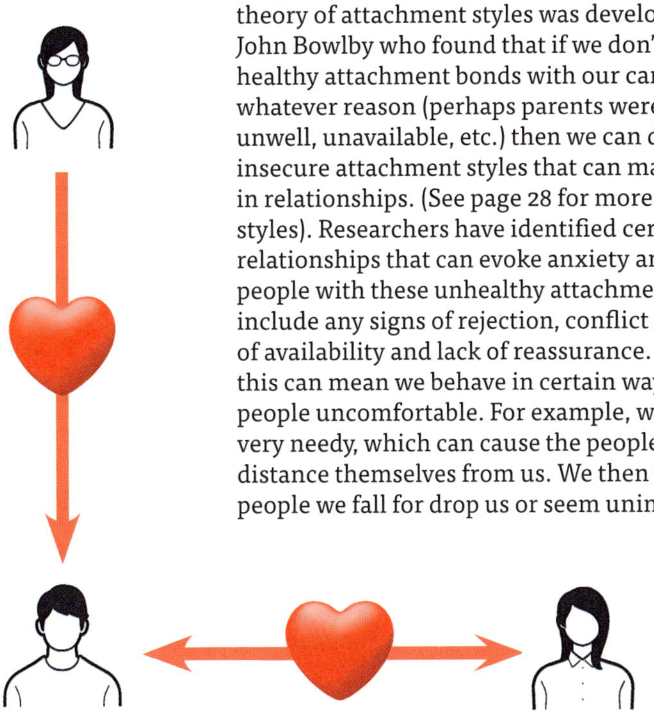

So what can you do about it? Here are some strategies.

FIGURE OUT THE PATTERNS: Take a good look at your past relationships and work out what it is that keeps happening, then look at the above explanations and see which one (or more than one) best fits.

BREAK THE CYCLE: Get your nervous system slowly accustomed to new patterns without it going into fight or flight; start making small changes in your life like eating new foods or taking different routes home from work.

SEEK HELP: Consider seeing a counsellor or getting support if you think you have low self-esteem. Cognitive Behavioural Therapy (CBT) can be effective at improving how you see yourself. Look at your own behaviours and try to identity if you tend to behave in certain ways based on childhood patterns.

Finally, if a relationship doesn't feel right, don't blame yourself or assume it's your own fault. Sometimes, it really isn't you – it's them.

THE HIDDEN SIGNS OF LOW SELF-ESTEEM

People with lower self-esteem tend to be more sensitive to signs of rejection in their partners, sometimes misinterpreting innocuous comments or actions as signs of disinterest. This then confirms their view of being unlikeable and also seems to keep them in the cycle of always attracting people who reject them.

People with lower self-esteem may be less inclined to undertake problem-solving actions, which can also contribute to repeated relationship failure. And finally, a 2018 study showed that people with lower self-esteem tend to engage in certain 'support-seeking' behaviours such as whining and sulking. These often lead to less, rather than more, support, which compounds the person's feeling that they always attract unsupportive people.

HOW TO MAKE SOMEONE FALL IN LOVE WITH YOU

So, you've met the person of your dreams, you've convinced them to go on a date...now all you have to do is get them to fall in love with you. Luckily, psychology has some great advice on how to achieve that.

In 1974, psychologists Donald Dutton and Arthur Aron conducted a fascinating study on two bridges over the Capilano River in North Vancouver, British Columbia, Canada. This was a great location because the two bridges were very different: the first one was a wide, solid wooden bridge with high handrails, only 3 metres (ten feet) above a small rivulet. The second one was the Capilano Canyon Suspension Bridge, which is 135 metres (450 feet) long, 1.5 metres (5 feet) wide and 70 metres (230 feet) above the river. Made of wooden boards attached to wire cables, this bridge sways, wobbles and tilts as you walk across it.

The 'wobbly bridge study', as it became known, involved an attractive female researcher asking men who were crossing the bridge to complete something called a Thematic Apperception Test. In this test, the man (who was assumed to be heterosexual – this was 1974, after all) was shown an ambiguous image of a woman that could be interpreted neutrally or in a more romantic/sexual way – a photo of a woman laughing, for example. The participant standing on the bridge was then asked to provide a back story for the picture – what did they think had happened or was happening? Their story was then examined for sexual or romantic content. The men were also offered the phone number of the female researcher, in case they wanted to find out more about the study.

The study found that more of the men on the scary wobbly bridge assigned romantic or sexual content to the pictures than those on the safe sturdy bridge. They were also far more likely to call the woman researcher afterwards – 50 per cent of the men on the wobbly bridge made the phone call, compared with 20 per cent of the men on the sturdy bridge.

What does this study tell us about falling in love? The men on the wobbly bridge would have felt far more fear than those on the 'safe' bridge. Fear is an emotional arousal mechanism and like all arousal systems, it can be manipulated. That means that if we don't know what is causing our arousal, we will cast around for an explanation. Sometimes, we might get it wrong and mislabel our emotions as a result. For example, we may mislabel fear as anger. In this case, the men were provided with an explanation for their emotional arousal in the form of an attractive person, so as a result, many of them mislabelled the fear they felt as attraction or even love. This is why so many more men on the wobbly bridge saw

romantic or sexual content in an innocent picture and called the female researcher later.

So if you want someone to fall for you, take them on a scary bridge for your date. If you don't happen to be near the Capilano Canyon Suspension Bridge, then anything that invokes a (healthy) fear reaction would work – a scary roller-coaster or a horror movie, for example.

This phenomenon also helps explain why there are so many office romances (a 2020 YouGov poll found that 18 per cent of Brits met their current or most recent partner through work). Of course, close proximity in a work environment helps, but working together on an exciting or stressful project induces an emotional arousal system that can easily be mislabelled as romantic interest. Not as much fun as a roller-coaster though – or even a wobbly bridge.

ARE YOU REALLY OVER YOUR EX?

Breaking up is hard, even if you know it's the right thing to do. It's even harder, of course, if it isn't what you wanted. There is often a lot of pressure to get back in the saddle and start dating again, but you may not feel ready. But how do you know if that reluctance is because you are not really over your ex – or just because dating again is such a daunting prospect?

Here are the signs that you are not quite over your ex:

- **YOU STILL COMPARE EVERYONE TO YOUR EX.** This could range from random strangers you meet in the street to colleagues or potential partners. If your ex is the yardstick against which you measure others (they are not as tall/clever/good at card games), you probably aren't over them yet.

- **YOU SEE SIGNS OF THEM EVERYWHERE AND IN EVERYTHING.** When everything reminds you of them, it has a deep effect on you. The weather reminds you of those romantic walks in the rain, an advert for a new film reminds you of a movie you went to see together, a certain cafe makes you think of their favourite lunchtime sandwich.

- **YOU GET EMOTIONAL WHEN YOU THINK OF THEM OR TALK ABOUT THEM.** If hearing their name sends you into a frenzy of despair, you probably aren't over them yet. If you can't talk about the breakup or even mention your life together without great distress, you are not over them.

- **BUMPING INTO THEM IS A HUGE DEAL.** You may invest a lot of energy into manipulating your routine so that your paths don't cross – or perhaps so that they do. Either way, your ex is constantly on your mind. You choose your outfit based on the possibility of seeing them or you go to a different pub at the weekend to avoid them.

- **YOU DAYDREAM ABOUT THEM.** If you spend a lot of time reliving memories about your time together, or replaying past events or conversations in your mind, you probably aren't over them.

- **YOU STALK THEM ON SOCIAL MEDIA**. You find yourself constantlychecking their feeds to see what they are doing and with whom. You torture yourself wondering if that attractive person they are with is a new partner, or if they seem happy without you.

- **YOU REACH OUT TO THEM – OR WANT TO – FOR THE SLIGHTEST REASON**. Your dog is ill? Brother got engaged? Got promoted at work? Your immediate urge is to send them a message to update them on your life. Perhaps you send the text, perhaps you don't – either way, this urge is a sure sign that you are not over them.

SIGNS THAT YOU ARE GETTING OVER YOUR EX:

- You no longer check their social-media activity to see what they are doing and who with. This means that your emotional attachment to them has finally loosened because you are no longer worried that they are moving on without you (and seeing someone new, for example). This represents a cognitive shift in your emotional attachment.

- You begin to get interested in new hobbies or in meeting new people. This shows that you are ready to reclaim your identity as someone separate from your ex and that you are ready to connect with parts of yourself that were set aside during the relationship.

- You no longer compare everyone, from random strangers you meet in the street to potential partners, to your ex. This shows that you are becoming more future-oriented and less wedded to the past.

- You stop ruminating about why you split up or where things went wrong. This shows that you have moved into a more accepting stage of the loss process. According to the Kübler-Ross model of grief, acceptance is the final stage.

- The urge to reach out to them for the slightest reason fades (you don't need to let them know that your friend got a new job). You're no longer battling the impulse to text them, stalk their social media or 'accidentally' bump into them. This shows that your impulse control is getting stronger as your rational brain is no longer being hijacked by strong emotions.

- You are no longer triggered by reminders of them or by seeing them. This shows that you are no longer in the 'fight or flight' mode where you see the loss as a threat to your wellbeing.

WHAT IT MEANS WHEN YOUR EX MOVES ON QUICKLY

You may think that if your ex finds a new partner quickly, it means they never really cared for you.

This is a common fear, but it may not be true. Sometimes a swift progression to a new partner suggests an insecure attachment style, and that they are struggling with the concept of being alone.

Moving on quickly may actually be a sign of how sad they feel about the break-up: they need to overcome these difficult feelings by finding a new partner who will make them feel better. They may also have self-esteem issues and need a new partner to make them feel wanted and desirable. Of course, there is also the possibility that they are 'moving on' in order to prove to everyone how OK they are about the breakup, in which case they are not really moving on at all.

WHY YOU'RE MORE ATTRACTIVE THAN YOU THINK

How attractive do you think you are on a scale of one to ten? Many people completely underestimate their objective attractiveness and rate themselves far lower than others would. Research suggests that many people, especially women, tend to judge their own bodies more harshly than their partners do. For example, a study in 2010 showed that women across a range of countries tended to think that heterosexual men prefer a far thinner female body type than they actually do.

This harsh self-judgement is especially true for the many people with body dysmorphia. They have a flawed perception of their body and may believe that their nose or some other body part is disproportionately large, despite it being objectively average in size. I see this a lot in my clinic. I have met clients who have worn face masks long after it was required during the Covid years or who constantly kept their face partially covered by their hands or hair, lest they reveal their supposedly hideous facial feature. I have worked with people who are convinced that their thighs are so unacceptably huge that they need to adapt their clothing and behaviour to shield others from the view, and I have seen perfectly lovely-looking larger people who are convinced that their body shape makes them highly unattractive.

The reason we underestimate our own attractiveness is that we tend to be far more conscious of our own flaws in appearance than we are aware of similar things in other people. Social media does not help in this regard, especially when we constantly see flawless, photoshopped images that our own raw selves simply cannot live up to. Research suggests that our self-esteem is lowered when we see photos of beautiful people and compare ourselves to them unfavourably.

We all have flaws in our appearance, but we often over-focus on them. For example, imagine you have woken up with a pimple on your chin. The more you look at it, the bigger it seems to get. Before long, it is as if your entire face is one huge, red, pus-filled spot. You then spend ages examining the spot from all angles, thinking about it, perhaps trying to figure out how to cover it up or deal with it. It becomes the complete focus of your attention. You are convinced that everyone else will find you hideous too. This is termed the 'spotlight effect' – the tendency to think that others notice our flaws more than they actually do.

We zone in on our imperfections, but other people see the whole person, in context. They don't focus on our flaws in the way we do when looking at ourselves in the mirror. When we speak to other people, we generally only casually scan their faces or body, focusing most on their eyes. In fact, we tend to be quite unobservant, which is why most of us make such poor eyewitnesses to a crime (How tall was the bank robber? What were they wearing? Any distinctive facial features? Err...). Sometimes we even fail to notice if a loved one is wearing new glasses or has a new hairstyle.

So a flaw that seems hideous to us will probably be barely noticed by other people. And that is why we are probably more attractive to others than we think.

IS SOMEONE JEALOUS OF YOU?

This may sound surprising, but we are not very good at knowing if someone is jealous of us. This is especially the case if we have low self-esteem, because if we don't think very highly of ourselves, why on earth would anyone else be jealous of us?

Yet I see many people in my clinic, especially young people, whose lives are blighted by the jealousy of others, but they are so caught up in what they perceive to be their own flaws that they just can't see it. Victims of bullying, for example, are often targeted because the bully feels jealous of them and then puts them down in order to feel better about themselves. Anyone who consistently displays bad behaviour or a bad attitude towards you may well secretly be jealous of you.

According to a 1989 study published in the *Journal of Social and Personal Relationships*, jealousy is made up of three elements – jealous thoughts, feelings and behaviours. Some people will experience all three or sometimes just one or two. Jealous thoughts include worries or suspicions, doubts, uncertainties and mistrust. Jealous feelings are those uncomfortable emotions we experience when we see or hear something that makes us envious. And jealous behaviours are the things we do as a result of our emotions or thoughts – checking social media feeds, questioning people, maybe even trying to control others.

These three elements can lead to giveaway signs that someone may be jealous of you. Here are some things to watch out for:

- Someone gives you back-handed compliments that are really barely disguised insults, such as, 'What a great haircut! It really hides your chin!', 'I love how you dress – you just don't care what people think, that's so refreshing' and 'It's really great how you don't mind working at that place.'

- They undermine your achievements or accomplishments. For example, if you get a promotion or a new job, they might point out the fact that it's not a very competitive industry or that the office isn't in a great location.

- They often compare themselves to you in a way that makes them sound better. For example, 'That's a great award you won – of course I won it two years ago.'

- They imitate you. A jealous person may try to be more like you, so watch out for someone getting a similar hair style or item of clothing as you, or taking up on of your hobbies or interests and then trying to outdo you.

- They are downright critical: someone putting down your achievements, having a negative attitude and being hostile may well say more about them than you. They may criticize decisions you take, choices you make, people you hang out with, your job...anything that they can find to be negative about.

- They try to upstage you: if you tell a story, they will tell a more dramatic one, if you mention going to a party they will have been to a more exciting one. They can't bear for anyone to admire you more than them, so always have to point out why they are better than you.

If more than three or four items of the above list remind you of how your friend treats you, maybe it's time to get a new friend. Real friends big you up, are proud of your achievements and want the best for you. Jealous people bring you down and make you feel there is something wrong with you – but it's not you, it's them.

HOW TO TELL IF YOUR FRIEND IS ACTUALLY A NARCISSIST

We hear so much about narcissists these days – everyone seems to be diagnosing their partner (or ex-partner), parent, sibling and friend with this personality trait. It's almost as if anyone who annoys us, belittles us or treats us badly must be a narcissist. Narcissism is the buzzword of the moment. But how do we know if someone is really a narcissist – or just toxic?

Narcissism gets its name from **Narcissus**, a hunter from Greek mythology. According to the myth, Narcissus was so obsessed with his own beauty that he couldn't stop looking at his reflection in a pool of water. He did nothing but stare at his reflection until he died.

While this label may be bandied about freely these days, psychologists agree that to actually be diagnosed as a narcissist, a number of traits must be clearly present. Toxic or unpleasant people lack these traits, and their annoying behaviour or attitudes are considered to be so on a more subjective basis. This means that not everyone will dislike these behaviours or consider them toxic. Narcissistic traits, however, can be objectively identified and someone who has enough traits to be officially diagnosed would be said to have Narcissistic Personality Disorder (NPD).

According to some estimates, between 0.5 per cent and 5 per cent of the population have NPD, with far more men than women being affected. *The American Psychiatric Association's Diagnostic and Statistical Manual of Mental Disorders*, Fifth Edition, has a list of nine criteria for this disorder, and someone must have at least five of them to receive a diagnosis of NPD.

NINE SIGNS OF NARCISSISTIC PERSONALITY DISORDER

1. A grandiose sense of self-importance.
2. A preoccupation with fantasies of unlimited success, power, brilliance, beauty or ideal love.
3. A belief that they are special and unique and can only be understood by, or should associate with, other special or high-status people or institutions.
4. A need for excessive admiration.
5. A sense of entitlement.
6. Interpersonally exploitive behaviour.
7. A lack of empathy.
8. Envy of others or a belief that others are envious of him or her.
9. A demonstration of arrogant and haughty behaviours or attitudes.

QUIZ: DIAGNOSING A NARCISSIST

The following quizzes will help you decide if your friend (or partner or family member) is truly a narcissist. Rate the statements below on a scale from 1 to 7, with 1 being 'totally disagree' and 7 being 'totally agree'.

Does your friend have these traits?							
	Totally disagree	Moderately disagree	Slightly disagree	Neither agree nor disagree	Slightly agree	Moderately agree	Totally agree
Score	**1**	**2**	**3**	**4**	**5**	**6**	**7**
1 They seem to have an excessive need for control.	☐	☐	☐	☐	☐	☐	☐
2 They seem to crave power.	☐	☐	☐	☐	☐	☐	☐
3 They appear to lack empathy towards others, so may say hurtful things or show little sympathy. They may even see other people's hurt feelings or distress as weakness.	☐	☐	☐	☐	☐	☐	☐
4 They seem very self-centred, always bringing conversations back to themselves.	☐	☐	☐	☐	☐	☐	☐
5 They come across as very selfish.	☐	☐	☐	☐	☐	☐	☐
6 They always seem to need excessive praise, admiration or validation. They may fish for compliments.	☐	☐	☐	☐	☐	☐	☐
7 They find it very hard to take criticism.	☐	☐	☐	☐	☐	☐	☐
8 They see themselves as superior to others and believe most other people are jealous of or envy them. If anyone is better than them, they may belittle them or try to diminish their successes.	☐	☐	☐	☐	☐	☐	☐
Total score:							

Does your friend have these traits?							
	Totally disagree	Moderately disagree	Slightly disagree	Neither agree nor disagree	Slightly agree	Moderately agree	Totally agree
Score	**1**	**2**	**3**	**4**	**5**	**6**	**7**
9 They seem to have a strong sense of entitlement, believing that normal rules don't apply to them, for example, or that they deserve special treatment or privileges.	☐	☐	☐	☐	☐	☐	☐
10 They can come across as very arrogant, frequently showing off or boasting, even exaggerating their achievements.	☐	☐	☐	☐	☐	☐	☐
11 They tend to be dismissive of the concerns of others, maybe even gaslighting them into believing that they are the ones in the wrong.	☐	☐	☐	☐	☐	☐	☐
12 They will happily betray betray or belittle other people.	☐	☐	☐	☐	☐	☐	☐
13 They lie, twist the truth or otherwise deceive in order to get what they want.	☐	☐	☐	☐	☐	☐	☐
14 They get angry easily, especially if other people don't do what they want or feel they deserve, or if they are criticized.	☐	☐	☐	☐	☐	☐	☐
15 They are preoccupied with knowing what others think of them.	☐	☐	☐	☐	☐	☐	☐

Total score:	

A score below 60 indicates a low likelihood that your friend is a narcissist. Scores above 60 suggest that it is possibly the case, while scores over 90 suggest a higher likelihood of their being a narcissist.

Narcissistic people have particularly negative impacts on other people and their feelings. This is why another way to help decide if your friend is actually a narcissist is to examine how they make you feel. See how much you agree with the following statements when thinking about interactions with your friend.

How does my friend make me feel?							
	Totally disagree	Moderately dsagree	Slightly disagree	Neither agree nor disagree	Slightly agree	Moderately agree	Totally agree
Score	1	2	3	4	5	6	7
1 Interactions with them make me feel mentally exhausted.	☐	☐	☐	☐	☐	☐	☐
2 They make me lack confidence in myself or my decisions or actions.	☐	☐	☐	☐	☐	☐	☐
3 They make me feel helpless, as if I can't do anything well or right.	☐	☐	☐	☐	☐	☐	☐
4 I feel like they are the ones controlling what I do or say.	☐	☐	☐	☐	☐	☐	☐
5 Sometimes after talking to them, I think I am going insane.	☐	☐	☐	☐	☐	☐	☐
6 I am often afraid of how they will react to things.	☐	☐	☐	☐	☐	☐	☐
7 I resent their lack of interest in me or my life.	☐	☐	☐	☐	☐	☐	☐
8 They make me feel inferior.	☐	☐	☐	☐	☐	☐	☐
9 I feel embarrassed about the way they treat other people, such as waiters in restaurants.	☐	☐	☐	☐	☐	☐	☐
10 I often feel confused and full of self-doubt after interactions with them.	☐	☐	☐	☐	☐	☐	☐
Total score:							

Scores above 50 indicate that your friend may actually be a narcissist.

DISCLAIMER:

These quizzes are not intended to be used to offer clinical diagnosis, as there are many factors that could impact scores as well as behaviours and motivations. They should never be used in isolation for any clinical or diagnostic purpose.

SUCCESS AND FAILURE

2.

THE SECRET FORMULA FOR LASTING MOTIVATION

We've all been there. All those good intentions to go to the gym, stick to that diet, finally write that report. We start off buzzing with motivation but it somehow fizzles out as other, more tempting pastimes (like staying in bed, eating chocolate or scrolling social media) push away our good intentions. This is demonstrated by the fact that over 90 per cent of New Year's resolutions are broken by mid-January. Can psychology help? Is there a secret formula to keep us motivated? Of course there is! More than one, actually.

Let's start with all those healthy new habits we want to adopt. Using The Health Belief Model (HBM), psychologists can predict the likelihood of your motivations for change actually sticking. The HBM was developed in the 1950s by social psychologists Godfrey Hochbaum, Irwin Rosenstock

THE HEALTH BELIEF MODEL

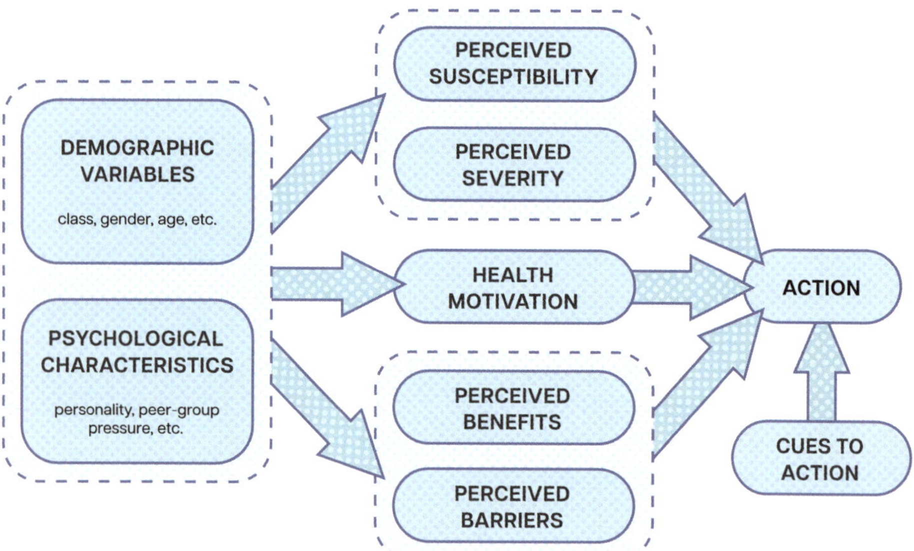

and others, who were interested in why people frequently failed to make healthy changes to their lifestyles, even when advised to do so by the Public Health Service in the USA.

The model states that a person's beliefs about the health-enhancing value of the change they plan to make tend to be weighed against the perceived costs of participating in this activity (time, money, quality of life). A range of factors are involved. Let's take losing weight as an example, as this is the most popular resolution people make, especially at New Year. According to the HBM, your chances of sticking to your new diet depend on the following factors:

- **Perceived susceptibility:** How likely you think it is that you will experience negative effects from not sticking to your diet (that is to say, how much you really believe your health or self-esteem will suffer).

- **Perceived severity of this outcome:** How serious you think these negative outcomes would be (you might believe that developing high cholesterol would not be so bad, but a belief that you might develop heart disease would be worse).

- **Perceived barriers/costs:** These include financial as well as psychological costs (such as the reduced quality of life that you might associate with the new diet).

- **Perceived benefits:** The benefits of looking better or being healthier have to outweigh the perceived costs.

- **Cues to action:** These are the things that can stimulate change, such as a toe-curlingly awful photo of your overweight self at the office Christmas party.

- **Self-efficacy:** How much you believe in your ability to actually stick to this diet. If you know you quit the last ten diets you started and you don't have much confidence this time either, you are doomed to failure.

The formula thus suggests that the person who is most likely to stick to their new diet is someone who is convinced that serious things will happen to them if they don't; has thought about how to manage the psychological costs of the new diet (by including pleasurable foods, for example); believes that there are immense tangible benefits to losing weight (looking and feeling better) which outweigh the costs; has had a 'cue to action' such as a health scare (or felt uncomfortably squeezed in an airplane seat) and who has confidence in their ability to diet (perhaps because they are trying something new or have strong social support).

Armed with this knowledge, you can increase your likelihood of sticking to your new way of eating by manipulating the variables in the model. Get a health check to get a real estimate of the serious consequences of a continued fat- and sugar-laden diet; make a list of all the benefits of losing

TRY THIS:

BACKWARD GOAL SETTING

The idea here is to start with your ultimate objective or goal and work backwards from there, figuring out each step you need to take to get to where you want to be. This approach helps ensure that every action and decision is aligned with the ultimate objective, making the process more focused and intentional.

1. **DEFINE THE END GOAL.** Clearly articulate the desired outcome. The goal should be specific, measurable and time-bound ('Launch a product by the end of next year' or 'Run a marathon in six months' time').
2. **IDENTIFY MILESTONES.** Break down the goal into smaller, achievable steps or milestones. Each milestone represents a significant progress point towards the ultimate goal.
3. **PLAN BACKWARDS.** Starting from the goal, determine what needs to happen immediately before achieving it, then continue working backwards to the present. This process reveals the sequence of tasks and decisions required.
4. **SET DEADLINES.** Assign timelines to each milestone to ensure progress is steady and measurable.
5. **ADAPT AND ITERATE.** Review the plan periodically and make adjustments based on new insights, obstacles or changes in priorities.

weight; minimize the psychological costs of the new plan; stick a spectacularly unflattering photo of yourself to the fridge (yes, this does work); and, finally, develop a strong belief in your ability to stick to the diet for a given period of time by following a realistic eating plan (perhaps one that incorporates real food, treats and social support). Of course, other factors play a role too, such as your personality, age and the people around you.

What about non-health behaviours? There are other formulae and models that can help motivate you in other areas of your life too, including Edwin Locke's 1990 Goal-Setting Theory. Locke's formula for effective motivation involves a step by step goal-setting approach:

EDWIN LOCKE'S GOAL-SETTING THEORY

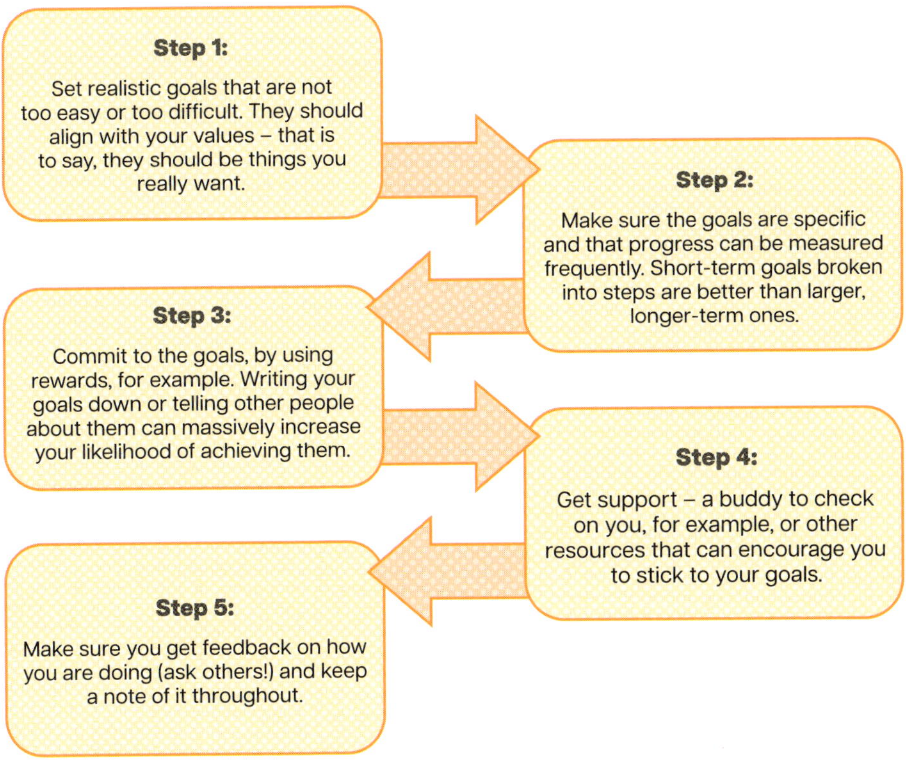

WHY PEOPLE PROCRASTINATE (AND HOW NOT TO)

Humans have always procrastinated, although the distractions of modern technology have probably made things worse. The concept of procrastination dates back to ancient Greece, where the philosophers Socrates and Aristotle referred to the act of doing one thing when you know you should really be doing something else as *akrasia*, which means 'weakness of will'. And *akrasia*, or procrastination, even happens when we know that we will be rewarded for doing the things we keep putting off, such as finally claiming back those travel expenses for work. Humans suffer from what behavioural psychologists call 'time inconsistency' or 'present bias': we value more immediate rewards (watching Netflix) over more distant rewards (being paid money we are owed).

We procrastinate for a range of reasons:

- **TO AVOID UNCOMFORTABLE FEELINGS**
  Stuff that makes us feel uncomfortable is stuff we tend to avoid for as long as possible. Tax returns make me anxious (I'm worried I'll make a mistake, plus there's the discomfort of seeing how much of my hard-earned cash I have to hand over). I find paperwork boring and unrewarding, while other people may put off making a phone call or avoid some other interaction due to fear or social anxiety.

- **LACK OF BELIEF IN OUR ABILITY**
  There is another activity I am procrastinating over which induces a whole different emotion: I have a huge canvas on which I have made a drawing in pencil, and now I need to start painting it. This should be an enjoyable activity, but I am scared of messing it up. I'm filled with self-doubt over my very amateur art skills, so I'm putting it off.

- **THE NEED TO BE PERFECT**
  If we feel that nothing we do will be good enough, we may not be motivated to even start. After all, why bother if we know we are only going to produce rubbish? Best not to start it – at least then we won't feel bad about what we have produced. Or maybe we should just wait until we feel inspired to produce better work...

- **DISTRACTION**
  This is a big one. There is so much out there to distract us, especially when the thing we are putting off is boring or less fun than the things that can distract us. Social media, for example, is far more likely to grab our attention than the bills we should be paying. Technology and the internet play a huge role here, but even doing the the ironing can seem a more attractive prospect than meeting that coursework deadline.

Here are some tips for how to break the cycle:

1. Break the task into smaller parts and make a start on the first bit.

2. Reward yourself for starting, as that's often the hardest part. Rewards could include some time spent scrolling social media or watching your favourite programme, going for a walk or getting yourself a cup of coffee.

3. Block out all distractions. This means putting away your phone, turning off or muting notifications, sitting in a space with minimal distractions (a library or a coffee shop or wherever works for you) or shutting the door to your office.

4. Use visual reminders and encouragers, such as to-do lists, wall charts, sticky notes – whatever works best for you. Seeing things in front of you and ticking them off or charting your progress can be rewarding in itself.

5. Have a 'procrastination buddy' or mentor who you can check in with and who will help encourage you to stay on track.

WHY YOU'RE MORE CREATIVE (AND THUS SMARTER) WHEN YOU'RE BORED

Boredom gets a bad press and is seen as demotivating. But did you know that being bored can motivate us too, and even make us more creative?

When we are bored, we lack neural stimulation. If our environment isn't stimulating enough to satisfy us, we may turn inwards to get the stimulation we need. Daydreaming has long been associated with creativity because it allows our minds to wander without our more conscious brains inhibiting us. So, wild meanderings or illogical ideas, crazy solutions to tricky problems and new ways to do things can all occur to us while we are daydreaming. And it is this that can lead us to become more creative.

TRY THIS:

DAYDREAMING

The next time you are stuck on a problem or just want to sharpen your brain, get yourself bored for a while. Do something that allows your brain to daydream. This could include:

- Going for a walk without listening to something on your headphones.
- Waiting in a queue without swiping or scrolling your boredom away.
- Looking out of the window on a train journey instead of working or reading a book.
- Staring at the clouds.

I tested this out myself with an intriguing study I carried out with a student of mine, Rebekkah Cadman. First, we made sure that our test subjects were really bored by getting them to either read or copy out a long list of telephone numbers. Then we gave them creative tasks to complete, such as coming up with as many uses for plastic cups as they could. We also gave them creative problem-solving tasks, such as setting them word problems known as remote associations. This involves giving someone three stimulus words and their task is to come up with a fourth word that can be combined with all three of them. For example, the answer to the three stimulus words 'measure', 'worm' and 'video' would be 'tape' (tape measure, tape worm and video tape). Of course, we also had a control group who did the creative and problem-solving tasks without doing the boring task first.

The results showed that the bored people were indeed more creative than the non-bored. They also revealed that those who had been given the reading-based task were the most creative of all, because writing can interfere with daydreaming (this is why we often start doodling during a boring meeting – it gives us extra stimulation without allowing our brains to daydream too much). Our study also showed that boredom led to better problem-solving in the remote associations task.

Good problem-solving skills are often associated with being clever or sharp – but being bored can also make us smarter!

THE SCIENCE OF GETTING PROMOTED (EVEN IF YOU'RE UNDERQUALIFIED)

Do you want to succeed at work, but worry that you are just not as good as other people? You may be surprised to learn that success is not always about being the best. Many workplace psychologists believe that while ability is obviously important to career success, there are a range of other factors that can make a difference in terms of being a top performer at work or not. So, if you want to outperform others, try these top tips:

1. **ATTITUDE IS EVERYTHING**
   Having an enthusiastic, can-do approach is vital to rising to the top. Some people, whatever their ability, are always seeking reasons for why they can't do something or why something won't work. Being the opposite can make you shine. No one wants to promote someone who is unenthusiastic, negative or who rubs people up the wrong way. Make sure that you are always personable and friendly and fit in well with everyone in the team.

2. **LEARN FOR LIFE**
   Smart people are always looking to gain more knowledge or skill. Attend as much training as you can, take on new tasks and learn from other people – even if it's outside your role. Everything can be an opportunity to learn.

3. **DON'T BE AFRAID OF FAILURE OR MISTAKES**
   Successful people take risks and accept that they won't always get things right. Being successful often means trying new ways to do things rather than playing it safe – and this can mean getting things wrong sometimes.

4 **DEVELOP RESILIENCE**

This means coping with knockbacks, dusting yourself down and carrying on. It means looking at how to solve problems when challenges occur, rather than being preoccupied with 'Why did this happen?'-type thoughts (see The why-how behaviour experiment on page 69).

5 **DEVELOP RELATIONSHIPS**

Nurture contacts and build networks. Treat everyone as important, because they are. Successful people learn from everyone and can never have too many positive connections in their life.

6 **HAVE THE CONFIDENCE TO ASK**

Many people are afraid to ask for a promotion in case they get turned down. It is indeed awkward to carry on if you have been knocked back, but belief in yourself and your abilities and that you deserve this promotion are vital. This self-belief can be contagious – if your boss sees that you believe you are good enough, they may be more inclined to agree.

7 **COMPILE SUPPORTING DATA**

A scientific approach means collecting and outlining all the evidence that shows why you should get that promotion – performance indicators, sales records, customer or colleague feedback, for example.

8 **DEMONSTRATE DRIVE AND WORK ETHIC**

Make sure that you work hard and that people notice you go the extra mile. There is no point being the hardest-working member of your team if no one knows about it. Be sure to drop your efforts into conversations and emails as reminders of your outstanding commitment.

9 **DO THE ROLE YOU WANT**

Step up to the role you want where possible, for example by filling in for your superiors when they are on leave or volunteering to take on one of their tasks. You could even ask to shadow them at times – all these things provide proof that you are up to the task.

HOW TO DEVELOP RESILIENCE

Do you want to be able to bounce back when things go wrong, cope with tricky situations and and better manage stress? That is what resilience is, and successful people have it in bucketfuls.

Resilience, or 'bounce-back-ability', has become a buzzword in recent years for good reason. Resilience is the capacity to recover from difficulties and withstand pressure, and it's a crucial part of dealing with all that life throws at us. Without adequate resilience, we can become overwhelmed by stress, feel unable to cope when things go wrong, struggle to see a way out of difficult situations, feel out of control and may even turn to unhealthy coping mechanisms such as alcohol, over-eating and avoidance.

THE TRIAD OF RESILIENCE

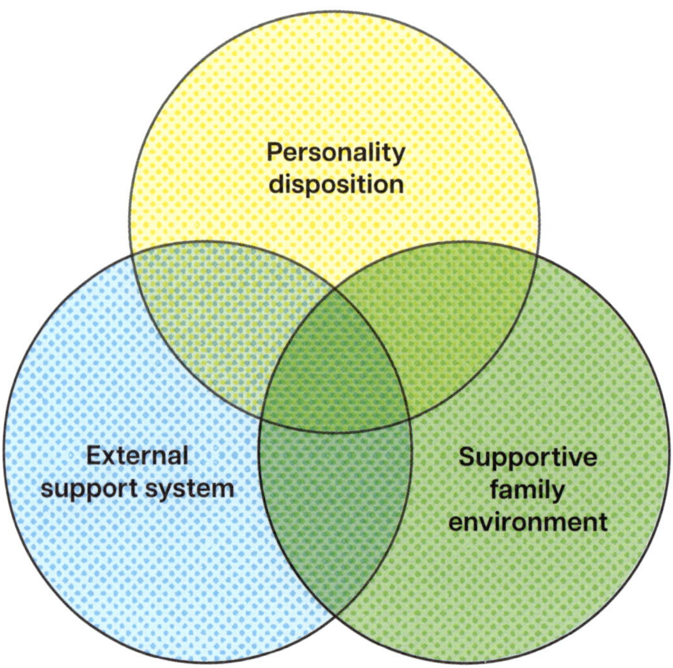

QUIZ: HOW RESILIENT ARE YOU?

This quiz will help you assess your ability to cope with stress, setbacks and challenges. Rate each statement below on a scale from 1 to 5, with 1 being 'strongly disagree' and 5 being 'strongly agree'.

Part 1: Emotional Resilience					
	Strongly disagree	Disagree	Neither agree nor disagree	Agree	Strongly agree
Score	**1**	**2**	**3**	**4**	**5**
1 I remain calm under pressure.	☐	☐	☐	☐	☐
2 I can manage my emotions effectively, even in difficult situations.	☐	☐	☐	☐	☐
3 I bounce back quickly after setbacks.	☐	☐	☐	☐	☐
4 I view challenges as opportunities to grow.	☐	☐	☐	☐	☐
5 I do not let failure define me.	☐	☐	☐	☐	☐
Total score:					

Part 2: Cognitive Resilience					
	Strongly disagree	Disagree	Neither agree nor disagree	Agree	Strongly agree
Score	**1**	**2**	**3**	**4**	**5**
1 I believe I have control over how I respond to life's challenges.	☐	☐	☐	☐	☐
2 I can find creative solutions to problems.	☐	☐	☐	☐	☐
3 I am able to reframe negative experiences in a more positive way.	☐	☐	☐	☐	☐
4 I focus on what I can control rather than what I cannot.	☐	☐	☐	☐	☐
5 I believe setbacks are temporary, not permanent.	☐	☐	☐	☐	☐
Total score:					

Part 3: Social Resilience					
	Strongly disagree	Disagree	Neither agree nor disagree	Agree	Strongly agree
Score	**1**	**2**	**3**	**4**	**5**
1 I have a strong support system of friends, family or colleagues.	☐	☐	☐	☐	☐
2 I reach out for help when I need it.	☐	☐	☐	☐	☐
3 I can maintain strong relationships even during tough times.	☐	☐	☐	☐	☐
4 I seek feedback and constructive criticism to improve.	☐	☐	☐	☐	☐
5 I feel a sense of belonging in my community or workplace.	☐	☐	☐	☐	☐
Total score:					

Part 4: Adaptive Resilience					
	Strongly disagree	Disagree	Neither agree nor disagree	Agree	Strongly agree
Score	**1**	**2**	**3**	**4**	**5**
1 I am open to change and new experiences.	☐	☐	☐	☐	☐
2 I can adjust my plans when unexpected obstacles arise.	☐	☐	☐	☐	☐
3 I stay optimistic even when facing difficulties.	☐	☐	☐	☐	☐
4 I believe I can grow stronger through life's challenges.	☐	☐	☐	☐	☐
5 I set goals and stay motivated even when facing setbacks.	☐	☐	☐	☐	☐
Total score:					

SCORING

80–100 POINTS – HIGHLY RESILIENT
You have a strong ability to cope with stress and setbacks.

60–79 POINTS – MODERATELY RESILIENT
You handle challenges well but may struggle in some areas.

40–59 POINTS – SOMEWHAT RESILIENT
You may find certain setbacks difficult but have room for growth.

BELOW 40 POINTS – NEEDS IMPROVEMENT
You may benefit from developing strategies to strengthen your resilience.

TRY THIS:

THE WHY-HOW BEHAVIOUR EXPERIMENT

Close your eyes and imagine you are leaving home to get to an important meeting. Imagine walking to your car, opening the door, getting in, feeling the car seat, thinking about the meeting. Now imagine putting your car keys in the ignition, turning the key and...the car doesn't start. You try again and it still doesn't start. Notice your thoughts and feelings as you ask yourself, why is this happening to me? Why me? Why can't I get the car started? What will this mean, what will happen if I'm late, what have I done to deserve this? Why does this keep happening to me?

Now refocus and open your eyes.

Reimagine the scene in the same detail up until the point that the car fails to start at the second attempt. Notice your thoughts and feeling as you ask yourself, how did this happen? How did the car break down? What was the sequence of events leading up to this point? How can I tackle this situation? What's the first step I can take to solve this problem? How can I get where I need to go?

How did each scenario make you feel? The second time, with the shift to 'how' questions, usually gives us more control and more positivity. We are more likely to solve the problem with a 'how' mentality than a 'why' mentality. This is resilience.

Here is how to develop your resilience:

1. Develop self-awareness of your strengths, weaknesses and values.

2. Embrace change – do things differently to mix things up a bit and get used to change. For example, take a different route to work, try different foods, speak to new people, get a new phone or piece of kit.

3. Catch and challenge negative or unhelpful thinking, such as catastrophizing.

4. When something goes wrong, focus on how to solve the problem rather on why it happened – see box on page 69.

5. Develop support networks of friends or family or work colleagues who you can debrief and offload to and who will encourage you to dust yourself down and pick yourself up.

6. Focus on self-care – exercise, healthy eating and getting enough sleep, rest and relaxation are essential tools to give you the strength to cope with adverse life events.

7. Develop persistence. Hobbies that require long-term commitment before success is realized can help develop the stickability that is the hallmark of resilience. Creative pastimes like painting, taking up crochet or knitting, learning a language, training to run 5k all are good ways to develop persistence.

8. Celebrate failure – things going wrong or badly sometimes is part and parcel of life. Accept failure as the route to success. This is the so-called 'failure paradox', which is the idea that failure can actually be part of success.

WHY DO I FEEL LIKE AN IMPOSTER? (AND WHAT CAN I DO ABOUT IT?)

Have you ever thought that a success you've had was a fluke? Felt as if you didn't really deserve praise, an award or achievement? Worried that people might find out that you are not as good as they think you are? If so, welcome to the world of imposter syndrome. And don't worry – you are not alone. Around 70 per cent of us feel like we are an imposter at some point in our lives.

The term imposter syndrome, or imposter phenomenon, was first coined in 1978 by clinical psychologists Pauline R. Clance and Suzanne A. Imes. According to them, the three defining characteristics of impostor syndrome are:

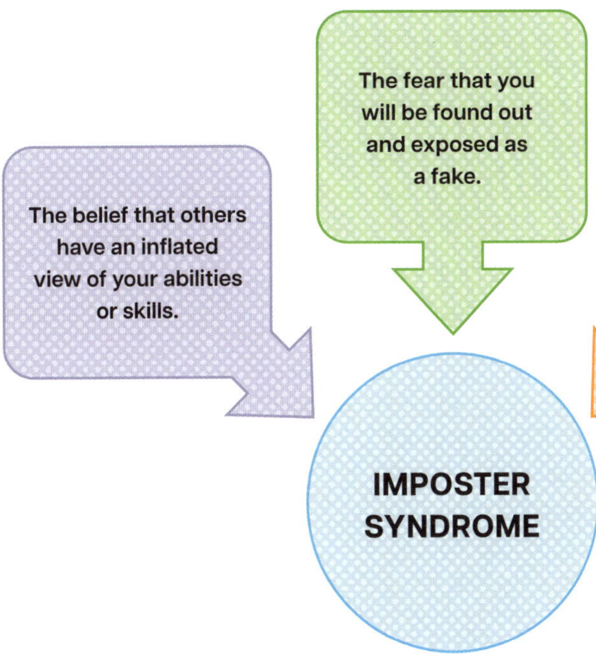

THE SYMPTOMS OF IMPOSTER SYNDROME

The syndrome is most common among successful people who, despite all the evidence, cannot believe that they are really good enough or deserve their success. This leads to a number of symptoms that can hold them back in the workplace and beyond:

1 **WORKING EXCEPTIONALLY HARD**
The imposter feels they must work with exceptional diligence in order to prevent their 'phoniness' from being discovered. Often this 'cover-up' strategy of hard work pays off and they feel relief – but then they start to think that they only achieved success because they worked so hard. This leads to feeling like an imposter once again: 'I'm not really good at this, I just work really hard.' So, the cycle of worry, hard work and temporarily feeling good continues.

2 **PERFECTIONISM**
In order for the imposter to prove their worth they must get everything right. Imposters therefore often fear failure or anything less than perfection, as this simply reinforces their view that they are a fraud. This perfectionism can lead to a cycle, whereby the fear of failure leads to perfectionism, which manifests itself in over-working or being unable to accept that a project is complete – or sometimes in being afraid even to start something for fear that it might not turn out perfectly.

3 UNDERMINING ACHIEVEMENTS
Instead of acknowledging the achievement that they have worked so hard for, imposters simply discount it as 'nothing special'. This is because the idea of achievement does not sit well with the imposter-ish belief that they are not really any good. The result is cognitive dissonance, where two beliefs (or cognitions) that contradict each other are held at once. To relieve the discomfort of this dissonance, imposters convince themselves that what they achieved wasn't so amazing after all.

4 DISCOUNTING PRAISE
On the one hand, the imposter desperately seeks approval and praise to validate their skills and talents, but when they receive it, they struggle with the contradiction that this creates: 'Why are people praising me when I'm rubbish? It must be that their praise is somehow worthless.'

All of these can lead to low self-esteem, poor mental health and burnout.

TRY THIS:

MANAGE THE SYMPTOMS

So, how can you overcome your imposter-ish feelings? Follow this guide:

1. Keep a list of your accomplishments – the actual facts. Put them in a table with the imposter-ish thoughts in one column and the evidence in the next (see page 74).
2. Come out as an imposter and get an 'imposter buddy' who also has imposter syndrome, so that you can boost each other.
3. Manage your social media: other people's 'perfect' posts can contribute to your imposter-ish feelings of not being good enough. Stop following people who make you feel like that.

TRY THIS:

REVIEW THE EVIDENCE

Write down your imposter-ish thought (I only got this job due to luck, for example). Complete the following table, in the style of the example given below:

The facts about my skills or qualifications that might have contributed to my success	My imposter-ish thoughts about that achievement	Skills, capabilities or talents that might have led to the facts
I received praise for a presentation I delivered	I didn't do it perfectly	It was a strong presentation with clear slides, delivered with enthusiasm

THE CASE OF THE ELEPHANT TIED BY A TINY ROPE: THE PITFALLS OF LEARNED HELPLESSNESS

One of my favourite anecdotes in psychology is the story of the elephant and the rope. All his life, the elephant had been tied to a stake by a rope tied around one of his legs. As a baby, he had spent many hours trying to pull himself free, but he just wasn't strong enough. After many months of trying, the baby elephant realized that there was no point in trying – he would never break free. So he accepted his fate, tied forever to the wooden stake with the rope. The thing is that adult elephants are a whole lot stronger than baby ones, and had he tried again as a fully grown beast to free himself, he would have had no problem. But he had given up early on. This is how huge elephants can be tied down with one relatively feeble rope their entire lives.

Unfortunately for the elephant, he had entered a psychological state of 'learned helplessness'. This is where animals (and people) learn that they are unable to do something and stop trying to do it, even when their abilities may have changed. This term was coined in 1967 by the American psychologists Martin Seligman and Steven Maier as part of their research on dogs and electric shockst first, the dogs were physically unable to avoid receiving electric shocks, but when they were later given a means of escape (by jumping over a barrier), they didn't bother because they had learned that there was no point trying.

Learned helplessness keeps us from trying things again that we have failed at in the past and keeps us stuck in failure. It can keep us stuck at work and at school, in bad relationships and in addictions like smoking.

The main symptoms of learned helplessness include:

- Feeling a lack of control.
- Failing to ask for help.
- Putting less effort into tasks.
- Lack of persistence.
- Giving up easily.

People in this state might benefit from some sessions of Cognitive Behavioural Therapy to help change the stuck mindset, but being aware of it and making attempts to change can be an important first step.

THE SELF-FULFILLING PROPHECY PUZZLE: WHEN PREDICTIONS SHAPE REALITY

A self-fulfilling prophecy happens when we predict something that then becomes reality – because we expected it to. There are two main kinds of self-fulfilling prophecy: those imposed on us by others, and those we impose on ourselves.

A self-imposed self-fulfilling prophecy might be if a person believes that they won't be able to pass an exam – they may feel it is not even worth trying, so indeed they end up failing.

THE PATH OF SELF-FULFILLING PROPHECIES

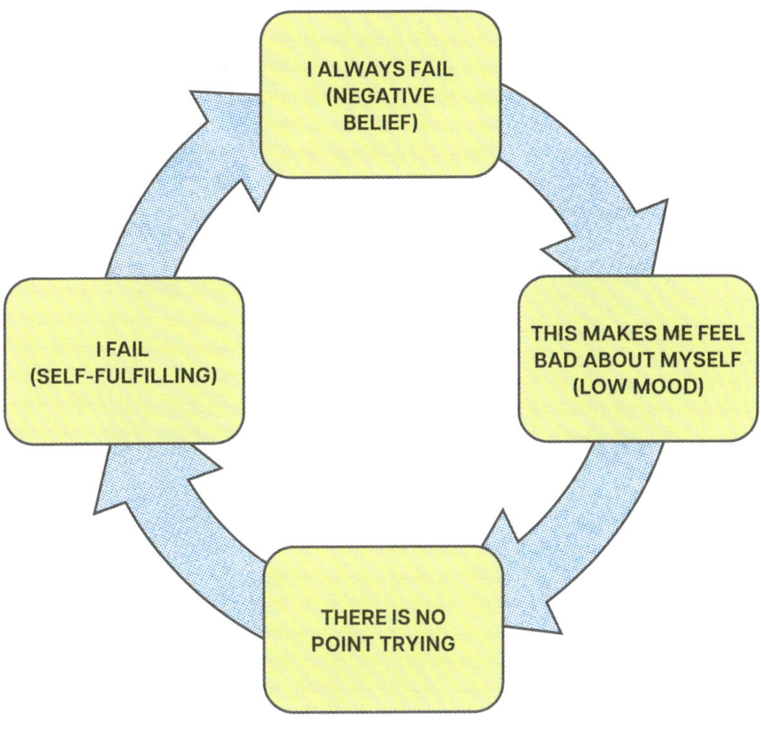

THE ORIGINAL SELF-FULFILLING PROPHECY

This term was coined in 1948 by American sociologist Robert Merton, based on his 'bank run' observation. There was a town where rumours began to spread that the bank was on the verge of collapse. This led to fear among the townspeople, who rushed to withdraw their money. This mass withdrawal led, of course, to the bank being unable to function, as it relies on investing customers' funds, leading to its collapse. The 'prophecy' of the bank closing actually caused it to close. We saw a similar self-fulfilling prophecy at work in the Great Toilet Roll Rush in the early days of the Covid pandemic in the UK. Despite there never being an actual shortage of toilet rolls at the time, rumours spread that there might be, causing people to rush out and stockpile huge volumes of the stuff. This, inevitably, led to empty shelves.

A good example of a common and perhaps more beneficial other-imposed self-fulfilling prophecy is the 'placebo effect'. This is when we are given a tablet that we are told will have a positive effect on our wellbeing. It actually contains no active ingredients, but because other people have told us things that lead us to expect this tablet to work, it does. It is thought that this is why some vitamin supplements or alternative therapies make us feel better – because we expect them to.

Self-fulfilling prophecies can impact other people's behaviour too. Research has shown that teachers who expect certain pupils to do well are often proved right, even when there is no academic basis for their raised expectations.

The opposite is also true: it is thought that teachers who have low expectations of pupils from certain ethnic groups or disadvantaged backgrounds (stereotyping them) end up creating situations where those pupils will do more poorly. This has been termed the 'Pygmalion Effect' and was illustrated in a study by Robert Rosenthal and Lenore Jacobson in 1968.

The researchers pretended to give students IQ tests and gave the supposed results to their teachers. They found that the teachers then put more effort into the students they believed had higher IQs, with the result that those students did, in fact, do better. These beliefs, imposed by the teachers, were internalized by the students and they began to believe in themselves more – meaning that they worked harder, and this contributed to their superior grades.

Thus, if we have high expectations of people, they tend to fulfil them – an important lesson for teachers and parents as well as employers everywhere. Low self-esteem can give rise to self-fulfilling prophecies – if we believe we can't, we probably won't. This can even lead to anxiety and depression. We may think we can't cope or are doomed to always fail, and these thoughts become self-handicapping self-fulfilling prophecies, which then lead us to feel worse about ourselves as we get trapped in a vicious cycle.

TRY THIS:

BREAK THE CYCLE

Avoid your own self-fulfilling prophecies by being aware of them. If you believe that things won't go well for you, you will probably act in ways to ensure that they won't. Be aware of other-imposed expectations, especially in your past, as these are often internalized and become your own. Catch yourself saying or thinking things like 'I can't do this, I will fail, I won't succeed' and stop the self-fulfilling cycle by acting as if you can do it.

SOCIAL MEDIA AND INFLUENCE

3.

WHY YOU CAN'T STOP CHECKING YOUR PHONE

When did you last check your phone? It you are anything like most people, it was probably very recently – some research suggests we check our smartphones every five minutes on average, and within five minutes of waking up (63 per cent of us sleep with our phone right next to us). We can't even walk down the street any more without our heads turned down towards the little glowing screen in our hands.

Whether we're checking messages, reading our newsfeeds or scrolling mindlessly when we have a spare moment, we just can't stop. Stanford psychiatrist Anna Lembke went as far as describing phones as 'the modern-day hypodermic needle', as addictive as heroin. But why are those little computers that we carry around all day so addictive?

- **DOPAMINE HIT**
  When you get a notification or see something interesting or fun on your phone, your brain releases dopamine. This is a neurotransmitter that gives a pleasurable feeling, making you want to repeat the experience (checking your phone) to get the next hit. And dopamine itself is quite addictive.

- **FEAR OF MISSING OUT (FOMO)**
  FOMO is much talked about these days and it really can have a big impact on how we feel. If we think that other people are having fun without us, we can feel excluded and lonely. This affects our self-esteem and we start to believe that we are unlikeable or unpopular. These are uncomfortable feelings, so we try to avoid them by constantly checking our phones to reassure ourselves that there isn't some major social event happening that we haven't been invited to.

- **HABIT**
  When we have been doing something long enough, it just becomes habit. Getting our phone out when we are waiting in a queue or on a train is just what we do, without really thinking about it. We may not even notice we are doing it. The peak times for us to habitually check our phones are when we are bored, stressed or switching from one task to another task.

- **ADDICTIVE DESIGN**
  Apps on our phones use sounds, images and other tricks designed to keep us engaged. Intermittent rewards (streaks, badges or levels), personalized content, notifications, social comparison, social validation (likes and comments) and a sense of urgency are just some of the psychological techniques used to keep us hooked – and many come from the world of slot machines and gambling. Facebook (now over 20 years old) even uses nostalgia to keep us engaged with its 'then and now' features that pop up regularly.

These are strong psychological processes, but can we resist their seductive powers? Here's how to break the addiction:

- **SEE HOW LONG YOU CAN RESIST THE ITCH**
  When you get that notification, it can feel like an itch that needs scratching – the urge to check it is immense. But you can train yourself to resist and eventually ignore that urge by making yourself wait to check your phone. Force yourself to wait...distract yourself with something else and see how long it takes for the itch to fade. You might be surprised.

- **HAVE A DIGITAL DETOX**
  Switching off your devices for any length of time might seem daunting, but it is a really good way to beat the addiction. Start with short periods of time – while you are finishing an important report or are out with the kids. Or choose activities that preclude the use of a phone, such as swimming or going to the theatre. You could also go for a partial detox by switching off or muting notifications. Build up to regular digital detox times, maybe even a whole phone-free day a week.

- **SET TIMERS**
  Putting boundaries on your phone use can help with the addiction too. But you have to be disciplined and make yourself get up and change environment when the allotted phone time is up!

AVERAGE ATTENTION SPANS

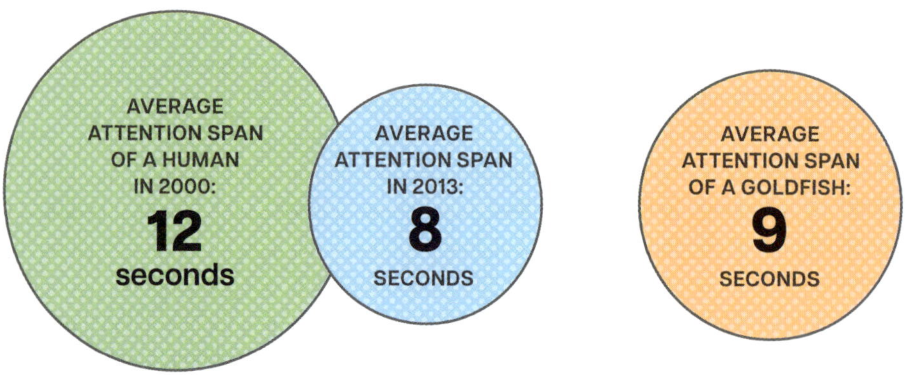

WHY OUR PHONES MAKE US MORE BORED

Despite all our swiping and scrolling, with endless entertainment just a few clicks away, researchers believe that up to half of us 'often' feel bored, with one study suggesting that we typically spend six hours a week feeling 'completely and utterly bored with life'. How so?

One of the biggest contributors to boredom is repetition and routine, and our lives these days are viewed and executed through a remarkably similar set of activities. We sit at our computer screen all day tap-tapping away, punctuated only by tap-tapping a smaller screen in our hands. Evenings are spent staring at a different screen. It's routine, repetitive...boring.

Not only that, but our phone allows us to live vicariously (and repetitively) via a screen. We watch videos, play games, read books, listen to podcasts, catch up with the news headlines, chat with friends – all via a glowing screen in our hand. That lack of interaction with the real world, with its smells, textures, tastes and 360-degree stimulation, becomes boring.

To try to counter that uncomfortable feeling of boredom we turn to...our phones. Instead of engaging in real-life activities, we hope that more scrolling and swiping will cure our ennui. The cure we seek makes the problem worse.

Our phones present another reason why they contribute to our boredom levels. Our brains are hard-wired to seek novelty; we even have a 'novelty-centre' in our midbrains called the substantia nigra/ventral tegmental area (SN/VTA) that responds to novel stimuli. When these novelty centres are stimulated, they cause a surge of feel-good dopamine to be released. In other words, we enjoy new things – we get a buzz from them.

Of course, once something has been perceived as novel, it quickly becomes old. We no longer get that buzz. But we crave that dopamine hit so we search for the next new things to give us that buzz. We constantly need new and novel stimuli to keep us satisfied. And as soon as we are, it is old – and boring. The more we refresh the page or log into another app in search of new stuff, the more bored we get of the stuff that we used to find exciting.

The solution? Less time on our phones and more in the real world. We need to use other means to un-bore ourselves and make sure that we have variety in our days. So, if you see me staring at the clouds instead of my phone while waiting for a train, you will know why.

THE PSYCHOLOGY BEHIND 'HATE-FOLLOWING'

Hate-following is the act of following someone on social media who makes us feel angry or jealous, or who we dislike. For example, following controversial characters or politicians or people whose opinions we disagree with, or spending time on sites that troll or say nasty things about celebrities – or even following our own 'enemies' or people we know and dislike in real life. But why do we do this?

Following people we don't like can give us the opportunity to keep an eye on them and reassure ourselves that we are doing better than they are. If the object of our hate does something sad or bad, instead of feeling sorry for them, we might rejoice in their misfortune. This all helps us feel better about ourselves. When it comes to celebrities, we might get a thrill out of posts that we consider cringe-worthy – and share them with our real friends so we can all have a laugh at their expense (and again, make ourselves feel superior).

Most of this stems from insecurity. We feel jealous of people we dislike and want to put them down in order to bolster ourselves. We may also want to keep finding reason to dislike them in order to confirm that they are bad people. Social psychologist Leon Festinger called this 'downward social comparison'. He pointed out that humans have a deep need to compare ourselves to others, and in fact, it is of evolutionary advantage to do so. Making sure we are acceptable to the tribe by constantly checking we fit in ensured greater protection than if we were cast out on our own. There are two main types of social comparison – upwards is when we compare ourselves to people we think are better than us, and downwards when we compare ourselves with those we think inferior. Downward social comparison makes us feel better than upwards, as it allows us to feel superior.

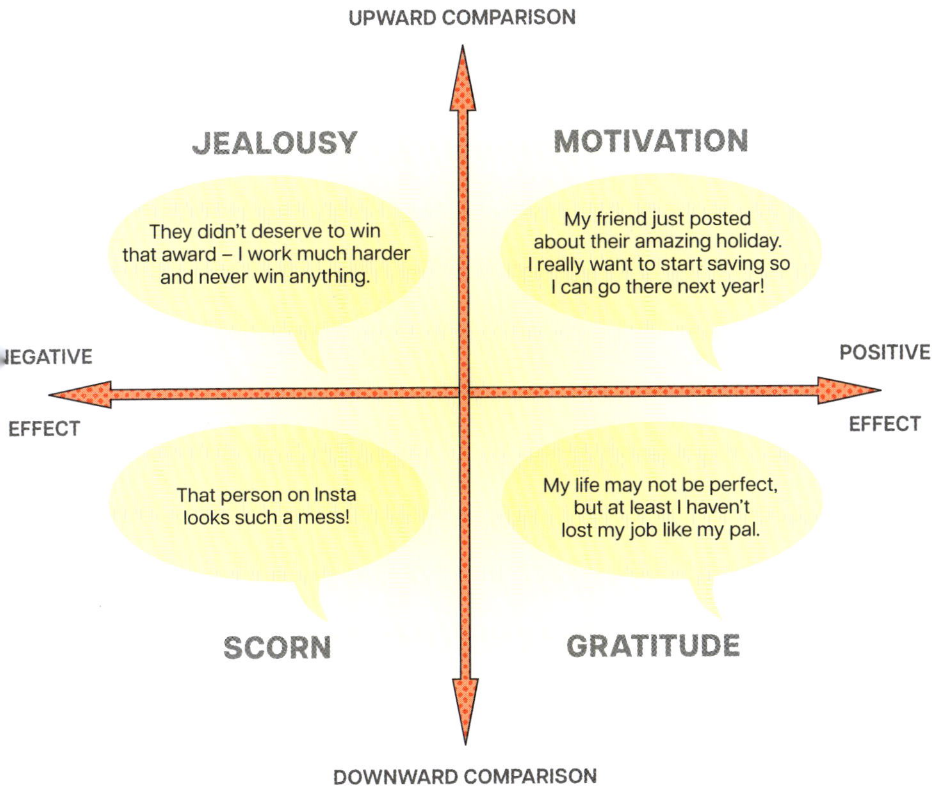

UPWARD AND DOWNWARD SOCIAL COMPARISON

Not everyone hate-follows out of jealousy, though. Sometimes following someone we hate can build as much of a connection as following someone we like; we get the same brain reactions and produce the same chemicals like oxytocin, dopamine and serotonin. These feel-good chemicals leave us wanting more – so we continue the following.

The problem is that we can get too embroiled in the hate-relationship and even become a troll. It is far healthier to follow people we like and have goodwill towards than it is to express hate. To rid ourselves of the habit, we need to look to other ways to boost our self-esteem and need for connection.

THE SECRET PSYCHOLOGY OF GOING VIRAL

It's a dream for many people. Imagine what it must be like to have a social media post go viral! To be shared and viewed by millions of people! Incredible! Well, the reality is a bit different. And I should know – it happened to me.

In 2018, I attended a conference – nothing newsworthy in that. But what the conference organizers printed on my name tag made me smile. They'd asked me which of my two affiliations I would prefer to have on the tag. I answered, and they took me literally. This is what the tag said: *Sandi Mann, Psychologist, Probably University of Central Lancashire*. I thought it would amuse my friends – so I tweeted it, complete with a photo.

At first there was nothing to suggest that this tweet would gain any exceptional attention. But after about five days, things started to go a little crazy. The first few retweets gained traction and it began to take on a life of its own. My phone was pinging constantly with retweets and comments, so much so that the battery began to die very quickly. Acquaintances began to message me saying they had seen the tweet in random places (not just on what was then Twitter) – the story appeared in the *Daily Mail*, for example. Imagine your phone sending you 40,000 notifications within a week! It stopped being fun quite quickly and began to take over my life. There were also hundreds of comments, many of them ridiculing my cracked fingernail, which was visible in the photo of the name tag.

And the thing with a viral post is that it never stops. Even when all the initial fuss dies down, it can flare up again, as a new generation stumble across it on sites like No Context Brits, Bored Panda and The Poke. And every time someone new comes across it, they share it...and it all starts up again. I fear I will never be free of this post, and it will follow me for the rest of my days! Consider this a cautionary tale.

9:58
Sandi Mann
@SandiPsych
Recently invited to speak at a conference and was asked which of my two affiliations I preferred to go on my name tag. Probably **University of Lancashire**, I replied. So that's what they put.
Sandi Mann
Psychologist
Probably University of Central Lancashire
525
7.8K
33K

THE NOT-SO-SECRET APPEAL OF GOING VIRAL

So, why do so many people dream of going viral? Despite the somewhat anti-climactic nature of my own viral tweet, I do get it. After all, before 'that' tweet, I was probably one of them. Here are the reasons why I think so many dream of going viral:

- **IT'S A THRILL**
  It really is – at first. The idea that little old me is making such an impact and reaching so many people is rather intoxicating. Most of us have very limited influence in the world, so a viral social media post can give a big dopamine rush at the idea of gaining such vast amounts of attention. Each ping on the phone gives another jolt of dopamine – it's all very exciting (though it wears off after about 500 pings).

- **IT OFFERS FAME**
  Everyone wants to be famous these days, it seems, and social media is seen as the short cut to achieving fame. Perhaps a viral post will allow you to achieve your ambition of becoming an influencer – and fame and fortune will follow. Sadly, none of that happened for me. I gained about 20 new followers, but fame and fortune definitely did not beckon.

- **WE CRAVE ATTENTION**
  This is perhaps the biggest factor for many. We increasingly live in a 'me me me' world, with everyone vying for attention. Getting attention means we are important, valued and validated. Lack of attention and being ignored means that we don't matter and don't count. Going viral on social media satisfies this craving for attention very quickly.

So, if you haven't been put off by my experiences, here are some tips from psychology that can help a post to go viral:

- Create a post that instils high emotion – such as humour or anger. People share things that make them feel, not that inform. My post was both funny and surprising.

- Create posts that people can relate to – something that they can imagine happening to them or to someone they know. My post was highly relatable as many people go to events where they get name tags, and it is quite easy to see how the humorous mistake on my name tag was made.

- Be quick off the mark with topical posts on current issues – poking fun at celebrities, politicians and current events always appeals.

- Introduce a twist – a surprising post with a vital twist can have real impact, especially if it also incorporates the previous ideas (relatability and topicality).

- Feel-good stories – people love a strong story of a real incident that makes them feel that the world is a good place.

Good luck – but be careful what you wish for!

HOW SOCIAL MEDIA CHANGES THE WAY YOU SEE YOURSELF

Social media can be a force for good – but also for bad. It changes how we view ourselves and that can affect our self-esteem. According to one survey in 2014, two thirds of people believe that social media sites make them feel inadequate about their own life or achievements. This can have a huge impact on our self-esteem, mainly because social media allows us to compare our lives, achievements and appearance with those of so many others. But the images we see have often been tweaked, and many social media feeds are tightly curated to present an unattainable level of perfection.

Social media is very good at showing us how wonderful everyone else's lives seem to be. Studies have found that frequent Facebook users believe that other users are happier and more successful than they are. Bragging and 'humblebrag' posts abound and every time we see images of that perfect holiday, toned body or glamourous event, we can't help but compare them with our own more mundane,

LOW SELF-ESTEEM AND SOCIAL MEDIA USE

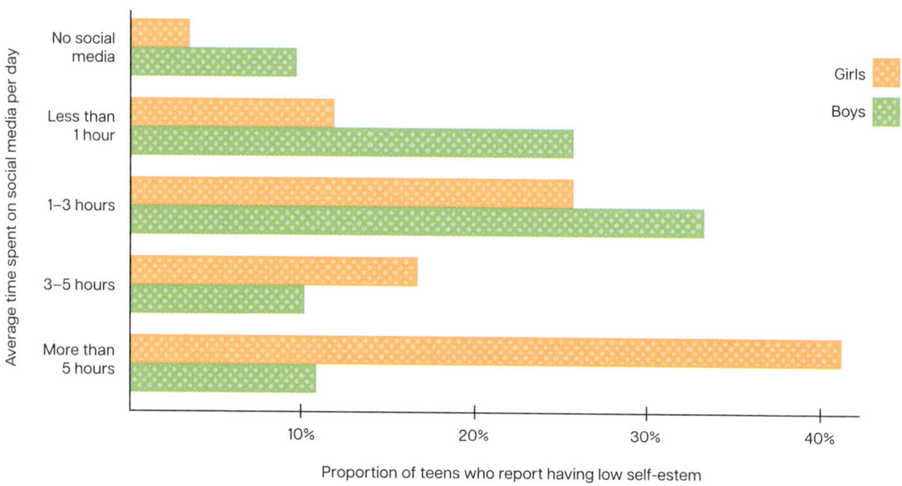

less perfect existence. Of course, most of these posts are highly edited (even Catherine, Princess of Wales famously admitted to editing her family snaps) so what we are seeing is literally unreal.

The other problem with social media is that it allows comparisons with a much wider range of people than previous generations would have experienced. Social comparison is an important human trait, but prior to social media, we would have compared ourselves to people who lived near us or who we worked with. Chances are that those people would have been fairly similar to us in terms of educational background and financial status. There would have been differences that might have fed aspirations, but these would have been relatively minor. We would have been less able to compare ourselves so intensively with people much richer or well-connected than us – we just didn't know as much about the minutia of their lives.

The social media generation of today can and do compare their lives with people in ways that was previously unimaginable – celebrities, influencers, royalty, film stars, sports personalities – the list seems endless. But it isn't just the rich and famous that we compare ourselves to. We look at friends and acquaintances and their own perfectly curated lives too. Thanks to social media, they and their lifestyles are in our face, constantly and continuously. Research suggests that approximately 88 per cent of people engage in making social comparisons on social media. If we don't measure up (and we won't, because their images rarely reflect reality) this is bound to impact how we see ourselves.

It isn't just the images that can change the way we see ourselves; the way social media fosters 'likes' and 'follows' can also impact our self-esteem. Social media constantly encourages us to seek validation of our views, opinions and lifestyle. We chase the likes and retweets as a way to measure society's approval of us; this is known as 'vanity validation'. Not getting enough of this can lower our self-esteem – and the lower our self-esteem, the more validation we seek to try to raise it. It becomes a vicious circle that only gets worse when we compare how many likes we get to other people.

ARE YOU 'AUTHENTIC'?

It is normal to present ourselves in different ways in different settings. As Shakespeare famously said, 'all the world's a stage...and one man in his time plays many parts'. We might be a parent, teacher, professional, daughter, sibling, friend, customer...each of these roles means we assume a different sort of identity. As a parent, there is an authoritative, wise identity. As a colleague at work, one defined by professional boundaries. We might resort to taking on a more childish identity when we return home to visit our parents, or we might become the 'fun' version of ourselves with certain friends.

Within all these different roles, we act differently. We might speak differently, using different words or tones. We might express different attitudes or political views. We might espouse different moral values. We might be extrovert in one setting but quieter and more reserved in another. In other words, each role has its own identity that allows us to fit in, be accepted, meet societal expectations or achieve our goals.

The problem with all these various roles and identities we assume in life is that it is easy to lose sight of who we really are. Which is the authentic self – the version we are with friends or the version at work? Who we are with a parental figure or with a romantic partner? Or maybe the real authentic self can only emerge when we are totally alone? Even the most basic aspects of identity, such as deciding whether you are an extrovert or an introvert, can be troubling if we know we can be either one, depending on the setting. It messes with our desire to be authentic – if we don't know what our authentic self is, how can we achieve authenticity?

The other issue is that we may have an idealized identity – the identity we want. This could be different from the identity that we think we have, and this disconnection can cause distress.

Feeling authentic is thought to be a vital part of mental health and can impact self-esteem. The mental effort needed to constantly present ourselves in an identity that is dissonant to our real one (because of peer pressure, or work demands) can get exhausting.

EMOTIONAL LABOUR – THE PROBLEM OF BEING INAUTHENTIC

Many of the identities we take on (or are obliged to take on) require effort to maintain. We frequently have to hide what we really feel or fake what we don't. For example, in customer-facing roles at work, we have to smile and be friendly, even if we are feeling miserable. At home too, we might have to put on a cheery face to the kids while inside we are crying. This type of effort, known as 'emotional labour', is thought to be a significant source of stress, especially if it is performed a lot. This is not only because of the hard work involved in maintaining various different identities, but because of the distress of not being able to present ourselves authentically.

QUESTIONING OUR IDENTITY

The 'father' of identity theory was German-American psychoanalyst Erik Erikson (1902–94), who proposed that adolescence is the peak time when we start to explore our identity in a process he called 'identity versus role confusion'.

At this age, we start to become more aware of the roles we play and start to question whether they actually fit our identity. As children, our identities tend to be internalized from our parents, but as we reach adolescence and grow towards independence, we seek an independent identity too. We may question our gender identity or sexual orientation, examine our commitment to a faith we have been brought up in, reconsider our feelings about a hobby or interest we have been devoted to for years. We start to challenge everything and try out new roles to work out who we really are. Identities can also be absorbed from those that others put on us: if our parents have attached a certain identity to us, such as being clumsy or selfish, that can become part of our self-identity, too.

This questioning process can continue all our lives, as our roles change over time – as we become partners or parents, take a job in this industry or that, or even when we are bereaved or retire. All these life stages involve redefining ourselves all over again.

In order to truly discover our authentic self, psychologists believe that we have to go through three processes.

1. We have to work out what we are good at, what we enjoy or where our skills lie. This often involves a process of trial and error that largely takes place during adolescence but can continue throughout our lives.

2. We have to choose our purpose in life. We all need meaning, and working out what we want to achieve forms a big part of how we see ourselves.

3. We then need to live in ways that allow us to fulfil our purpose and utilize our skills well or that allow us to gain enjoyment and fulfilment. Choosing (and re-choosing) a career, a place to live or a partner, for example, are all part of this process.

THE BAADER–MEINHOF PHENOMENON: WHY SOMETHING WE'VE JUST HEARD ABOUT APPEARS EVERYWHERE

Have you ever come across a new term or made a new discovery, only for it to then crop up seemingly everywhere? It could be a word, a breed of dog, a scientific fact...whatever it is, as soon as you learn about its existence, it suddenly seems to pop up all over the place. After reading this, you may well start coming across mentions of the Baader–Meinhof phenomenon. This term dates back to 1994, when an American man named Terry Mullen wrote about having encountered references to the 'Baader–Meinhof gang' twice in the space of 24 hours. This West German far-left militant group, also known as the Red Army Faction, was mainly active in the 1970s and hadn't made the news in the US in years. Although Mullen was intrigued by this coincidence, what he was experiencing was a frequency illusion.

Once we become aware of something, we start to notice it more – we think that the object in question is popping up more frequently, but really, it is just that we are now paying more attention to it. This is sometimes also called the red car phenomenon: you decide to buy a red car in order to stand out more, and suddenly everywhere you look there are red cars. Of course, there are no more red cars in the world than there were before you bought yours – you are just noticing them more now.

Two psychological processes are at play with the Baader–Meinhof phenomenon: selective attention and confirmation bias. Selective attention means that we notice or pay more attention to some things than others, while confirmation bias is when we look for pieces of evidence to support our beliefs while rejecting and not noticing those that don't. With the Baader–Meinhof phenomenon, we unconsciously look for more examples of the new idea (because our brain pays more attention to something new) and when we find them, this confirms our belief that they are increasing in frequency.

Of course, with the advent of social media algorithms, it is possible that we are now experiencing the opposite of the Baader–Meinhof phenomenon when our interest in a product sees our social media pages flooded with adverts for it. In this case, there probably really is a proliferation of these images or words – the electronic 'spies' have noticed your interest via Google searches, email mentions and possibly even by listening to your conversations, and the marketing algorithms have done the rest.

WHO DO WE TRUST?

Even in today's more impersonal and less trusting society, we have to make decisions about who to trust all the time. We might have to trust someone to give us accurate directions, to make a recommendation for a product, to provide a good service, to watch our bag on a train or any other of the many ways we rely on trust. How do we decide who is trustworthy and who isn't? It turns out that psychology has the answer.

Research into who we trust is often considered to be part of the science of social influence and is often used to help marketing experts build up trust in a brand or product. In the 1980s, Robert Cialdini, Regents' Professor Emeritus of Psychology and Marketing at Arizona State University, suggested a number of factors that will increase our trust in a person:

- **CONFIDENCE:** We are more likely to trust someone who appears confident and competent. This is why so many brands use experts to sell a product – the dentist in the white coat in a toothpaste ad, for example. The white coat creates an aura of confidence and competence, but just knowing that experts recommend a product may be enough for us to trust it being the best. Using scientific or medical terms can also enhance confidence and competence – and hence our trust. Manufacturers of beauty products employ this technique all the time, referencing 'microencapsulated peptides' or 'activating skin's natural collagen production'.

- **SIMILARITY:** We trust people who are like us. This is explains the rise of the 'ordinary influencer'– brands know that we are more likely to trust someone's recommendation to buy a product if we feel they are similar to us. In the same vein, many household products are sold by actors playing the role of a mum or dad, which makes them just like us.

- **LIKEABILITY:** We trust people we like. Thus, brands will often use popular celebrities or likeable personalities to sell their products.

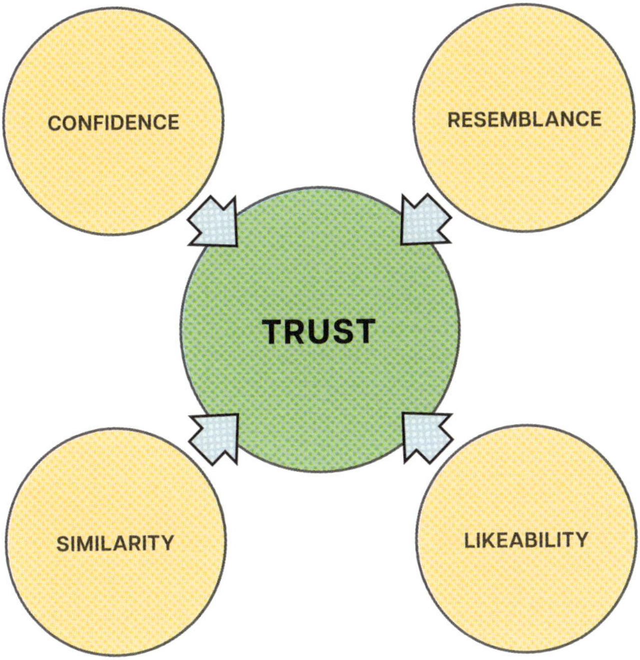

FACTORS THAT INCREASE TRUST

- **RESEMBLANCE TO OTHERS WE HAVE TRUSTED:** Research in 2018 found that we are more likely to trust someone who looks like a person we have trusted in the past. So if someone on a previous train journey proved reliable in watching our laptop while we nipped to the loo, on our next journey we are likely to seek out someone who looks like that first person.

THE TRUST HORMONE

Did you know that there is a trust hormone? Research shows that when other people show trust towards us, we produce oxytocin, sometimes called the love or affiliation hormone. And, when our oxytocin levels are higher, we are more likely to trust others. We actually produce more oxytocin when we are stressed than when we are relaxed. This is probably because when we are stressed and unhappy, we need to build bonds with others to help us get the social support we need.

THE DARK SIDE OF THE MIND

4.

HOW TO SPOT A LIAR (AND AVOID BEING FOOLED)

If I were to ask you what clue might reveal that someone is lying to you, you'd probably say some variation of 'scratching their nose' or 'not looking me in the eye'. Yet these are actually fairly unreliable ways to spot a fibber, despite popular belief. In general, we are pretty bad at telling when people are lying to us – research suggests that even with training, we do only slightly better than chance. This is partly because any fibber worth their salt will know the popular myths about lie detection, and therefore make sure to maintain steady eye contact and avoid touching their nose while feeding you their lies.

So how can you spot a liar? Fortunately, there are some more dependable cues that can decrease your chance of being made a fool of:

1. **BODY LANGUAGE**
   Keeping a careful eye on body language is vital but there is no single tell-tale sign – like nose scratching – to look for. Instead, watch out for a mismatch between what the person says and their body language: saying 'no' but slightly nodding their head, talking calmly but tapping their fingers, saying something positive while frowning, for example.

2 CHANGES IN TONE OR BODY LANGUAGE

If you can get a 'baseline' of how someone speaks and presents themselves when they are telling the truth, you can use this to compare with how they are when they might be lying. So have a general chat before asking them the key questions and watch for changes in demeanour.

3 AVOIDING THE WORDS 'I', 'ME' OR 'MY'

If someone is recounting a story or incident they are lying about, their avoidance of 'I' may show that they are trying to distance themselves from the account.

4 STRUGGLING TO RECOUNT EVENTS IN A DIFFERENT ORDER

They might be able to tell a tall story from start to end (chronologically) but be unable to cope with telling it out of sync.

5 USE OF PASSIVE RATHER THAN ACTIVE VOICE

For example 'Having a coffee with her is a favourite activity' (passive) rather than 'I enjoy having coffee with her' (active). The use of the passive voice can indicate that the liar is trying to distance themselves from their shifty tale.

6 REPETITION OF KEY WORDS AND PHRASES

Liars are so busy concentrating on keeping their story straight that they might resort to using phrases or words such as 'you know', 'like' and 'believe you me' more often than usual.

7 PAUSES

Long pauses before answering a question could be indicative of someone having to think far too much to come up with something to say. Similarly, repeating questions before answering them can buy someone extra thinking time.

8 CONTRADICTIONS

A great way to spot a liar is if they trip themselves up by saying something contradictory or talking in the wrong tense. Such as saying 'whenever I see her…' when they have previously claimed not to have seen her for ages.

9 CHANGING TENSE

If they change tense part-way through their story, this may indicate some confusion (and a struggle to keep the lie going) or that they are stressed and cognitively overloaded with remembering the lie. For example, 'we left the house and got in the car…we're driving along and suddenly we see a man'.

10 OVER-REASSURANCE

A liar may make too much effort to convince you that they are being truthful. Phrases such as 'I'm telling the absolute truth' or 'to be perfectly honest' might set alarm bells ringing.

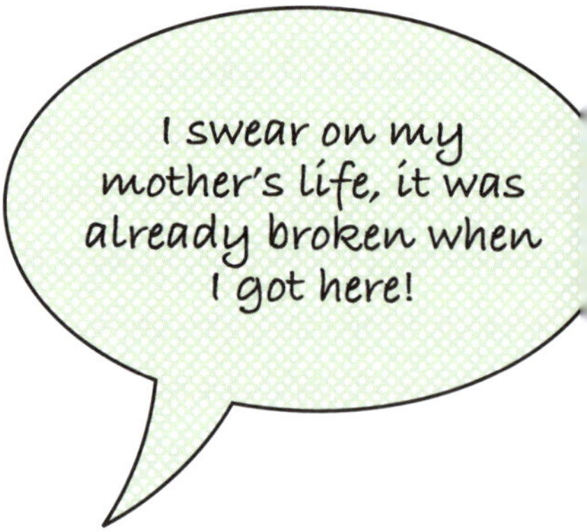

THE PSYCHOLOGY OF REVENGE (AND WHY IT FEELS SO GOOD)

An intriguing Swiss study from 2004 showed that when we think about revenge, we experience an increase in neural activity in the caudate nucleus, an area of the brain known to be associated with reward. This really demonstrated the age-old concept that 'revenge is sweet'. Revenge, supposedly, feels good, and it seems we are hard-wired to exact a fitting punishment on those who have wronged us.

From an evolutionary perspective, revenge made sense in that it prevented others taking advantage of you. Person A would be wary of stealing food from Person B in case Person B took their revenge and destroyed their house. Revenge and the threat of revenge helped keep law and order and gave us a better chance of keeping the stuff that would help us survive. But what about today? Does revenge always help?

Nowadays, psychologists find that taking revenge does not always make the avenger feel better. Worse than that, it can often start a cycle of vengeful behaviour, as the other person in turn takes their revenge on the avenger and so on. Disputes lasting generations can start this way, as well as all manner of negative behaviours with lasting consequences. Despite this, revenge is still popular, even if we know it is not wise. Why do we have such a thirst for revenge?

Social psychologist Mario Gollwitzer suggests two theories about why we find revenge satisfying. The first is 'comparative suffering' – the idea that revenge restores the natural order in the form of justice. According to this theory, it shouldn't matter who exacts the revenge, as long as the offender suffers. And we do sometimes delight in 'karma' when we feel the world has taken revenge on our enemy for us.

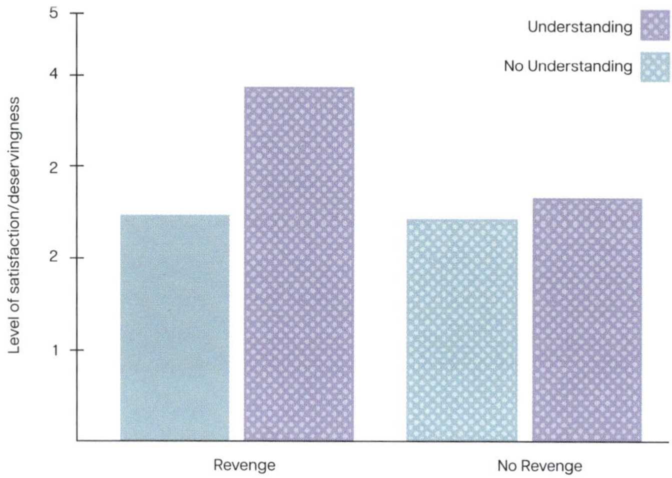

THE UNDERSTANDING HYPOTHESIS

The other theory is the 'understanding hypothesis', which suggests that the offender suffering is not enough – they also have to understand the link between the misfortune that has befallen them and the wrong they did. In this case, 'karma' would not suffice, and more direct action would be needed for someone to feel fully avenged. It's not just about payback, but about conveying that the initial behaviour was unacceptable. Only then can the wronged party feel satisfied.

The problem is that this message is often not delivered to or fully accepted by other party. This leads to the person seeking revenge still feeling angry – and worse, it leaves the other person feeling that they have been unjustly treated. If I don't understand or accept why you did somehing to me, I will probably be angry – and will want my revenge on you! And so the cycle continues. Revenge is thought to be a motivating factor in around 20 per cent of murders in the developed world. Revenge is definitely not as sweet as it may seem.

HOW TO KNOW IF SOMEONE IS MANIPULATING YOU

It is human nature to want to influence others to do what we want or believe is best – I think this restaurant is better than your preferred option, so will try to persuade you to go there instead of to your (in my view) inferior choice.

I might try to persuade you with logic and sound arguments ('It has a wider range of dishes and the seats are more comfortable') or with bartering ('Let's go to my choice this time, and yours next time'). But if I try to use more sneaky tactics, I might be guilty of manipulation. For example, I might sulk if you don't agree with me, or refuse to talk to you. I might even trick you by pretending to go along with your choice and then 'discover' that your preferred restaurant is all booked up. I might even gaslight you by trying to convince you that you don't like your preferred restaurant after all – perhaps by referring to false memories of poor service ('What do you mean you don't remember?'). I might threaten or emotionally blackmail you – 'Fine, we will go to the place you want to go to, but it will be your fault if I am up all night with stomach ache after eating their food.'

All of this is manipulation – the act of trying to get someone to do something with underhand, coercive or controlling methods. It can happen in any type of relationship, be it with a romantic partner, friend or work colleague.

Signs that someone is trying to manipulate you include:

- Making you feel guilty.
- Encouraging you to doubt yourself.
- Making you distrust your own ability to make decisions.
- Comparing you unfavourably to others.
- Giving ultimatums.

- Blaming you for things you haven't done.
- Gaslighting you into questioning your own reality.
- Using exaggeration to convince you.
- Sulking or give you the cold shoulder if you don't agree.
- Oscillating between cruel behaviour and love-bombing.

Unfortunately, some people are always going to be more prone to manipulation than others. Manipulators thrive on what they see as the weaknesses that make someone vulnerable to their underhand tactics. So, as well as looking for common signs in the manipulator, watch out for these signs that you might be vulnerable to manipulation:

- You are a people pleaser and making others happy is what you do best – even at the expense of your own happiness (which doesn't matter as much).
- You see the best in other people and make excuses for their bad behaviour.
- You find it difficult to say no to things even if you want to.
- You are always trying to get approval and validation from other people.
- You don't trust yourself to make the right decisions or do things the right way.
- If something goes wrong in a relationship you tend to blame yourself.

If you think this is your personality type and that you are being manipulated, take a step back. Put boundaries in place about what you do and do not want to do, and stick to them. Learn to say no. Start trusting yourself more – and remember that it's OK to get it wrong sometimes. Everyone does.

'No' is a complete sentence.

THE STRANGE SCIENCE OF SELF-SABOTAGE

Have you ever really wanted to achieve something, but just as you are close to the finishing line, you deliberately did something that undermined all your efforts and led to failure? For example, you studied really hard for an exam, only to stay up till 3am the night before watching Netflix. This is self-sabotage (sometimes called self-handicapping), and it is more common than you may think.

Self-sabotage is strange – why would we want to work so hard then do something to ruin it all? Of course, we are not always consciously self-sabotaging; sometimes we are not aware that this is what we are doing. But it is still negative behaviour that undermines our values and attempts to reach our goals. Why do we do it?

There are many different kinds of self-sabotage, ranging from the obvious to the very subtle, including:

- **PROCRASTINATION**
  Putting off tasks that need to be done to achieve the success you crave.

- **SELF-MEDICATION**
  Turning to alcohol or drugs instead of facing challenges or difficulties (going on a bender the night before a job interview, for example).

- **PERFECTIONISM**
  Not letting a task be completed until it is 'perfect'.

- **COMFORT EATING**
  Turning to unhealthy eating patterns even though you are trying to make healthier choices (for example, having a binge after managing to lose some weight).

The reasons we sabotage our own success are varied:

- **FEAR OF SUCCESS**
  Sometimes we think we want to succeed but actually deep down, we are afraid of it. Success can bring changes, new responsibilities, greater expectations and new challenges. For example, I often have patients who start responding well to treatment and then self-sabotage, perhaps by turning to drugs or by saying they are unable to progress. It can be that they are afraid of what being better might mean – they might have to leave the house, get a job, face people, manage on their own or deal with difficult situations. All manner of things that, in their current state, they don't have to face. By self-sabotaging, they can avoid the consequences of success.

- **FEAR OF FAILURE**
  The other side of the fear of success is the fear of failure. If I have an important job interview tomorrow, how will I feel if I don't get the job? It will make me feel rubbish and I am afraid of that feeling. Perhaps it would be better if I sabotage my chances so at least I will have something on which to blame my failure. It's not that I am rubbish, it's that I was hungover. If only I hadn't gone out drinking, I might have got the job!

- **LOW SELF-ESTEEM**
  If you don't think you are good enough to succeed, it can be very uncomfortable when you do, in fact, start to succeed. The belief that you may have held all your life of not being good enough is now being threatened by the evidence. Even though part of you yearns to be 'good enough', the feeling of not being good enough is familiar and thus feels safe. You self-sabotage to keep yourself in that safe, familiar space.

- **LOW SELF-WORTH**
  Slightly different from self-esteem, self-worth is to do with being worthy of good things and succeeding. If you have been brought up to feel that you are a bad, undeserving person, being on the brink of success may make you uneasy. You may start to worry that you don't deserve this and so had better do something about it, so that you don't get what you are not worthy of.

So, if you find yourself constantly wanting to do X but doing Y instead, try to catch any thoughts that might indicate there is self-sabotage going on. Thoughts such as 'there's no point trying, I will only fail', 'I am not sure I want to succeed' and 'I am not good enough' are all signs that you should challenge your need to self-sabotage.

CAN YOU REALLY READ MINDS?
THE SUBCONSCIOUS CUES WE ALL MISS

The most frequent comment a psychologist hears when revealing their profession is 'So, can you read my mind?' It is a common misperception that psychologists can read minds, but in a way, it is partly true. Of course, no one can actually read someone else's mind, but there are many tricks that psychologists learn that can provide clues to what someone is thinking.

Reading minds involves close observation of body language, demeanour, words and para-language in order to build up clues as to what a person is really thinking. Here are some top tips:

- **UNDERSTAND NONVERBAL CUES**
  Body language, facial expressions and gestures are powerful indicators of someone's thoughts and emotions. Watch out, in particular, for what social psychologist Paul Ekman called microexpressions. these are brief, involuntary facial expressions, such as a fleeting smile or frown, that can reveal someone's true feelings, even if they are trying to hide them.

- **OBSERVE POSTURE AND GESTURES**
  Watch out for crossed arms that might signal disagreement, while leaning forward can show interest or engagement.

- **LISTEN FOR THE PARA-LANGUAGE**
  This is all the sounds and utterances someone makes other than the actual words they speak. Sometimes these can contradict what they are saying, so hidden meanings can be uncovered. For example, a change in tone or pitch might indicate excitement, fear or doubt.

THE ONE MILLION DOLLAR CHALLENGE

Mind-reading is also called telepathy and many entertainers and magicians claim to be able to do this. James Randi (1928–2020), also known as The Amazing Randi, was a Canadian-American magician, sceptic and scientific investigator known for debunking paranormal and pseudoscientific claims. He famously issued his 'One Million Dollar Challenge' to anyone who could demonstrate evidence of a supernatural ability, including telepathy, under controlled scientific testing conditions. None of the one thousand people who applied won the prize money.

THE SCIENCE BEHIND RIVALRIES (AND WHY YOU SHOULD HAVE ONE)

A rival, by definition, is someone who is competing with us for something. This could be a sporting rivalry, a personal rivalry at work, a sibling rivalry or someone competing with you for someone else's attention. Either way, we may feel we hate our rivals, but there can be benefits to having them.

The science of rivalries is rooted in social-identity theory, which suggests that people gain self-esteem from being part of a group. This theory, first proposed in the 1970s by social psychologists Henri Tajfel and John Turner, suggests that belonging to groups helps us develop our sense of self and that competition between groups strengthens that even more. Belonging to an 'in-group' like a football team, family, work group or friendship group, can give us a sense of pride, belonging and purpose.

When there is a rival group (an 'out-group'), we tend to invest time and effort into bolstering our own group identity while minimizing theirs. This is well illustrated by football chants denigrating the opposition – joining in with such chants strengthens our own in-group bond and makes us feel good.

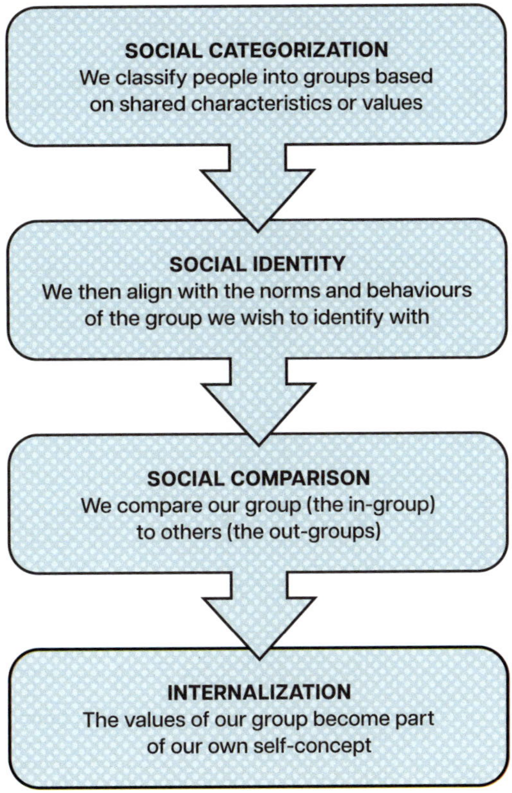

SOCIAL IDENTITY THEORY

Group or personal rivalries can enhance our own performance because we have to work harder to win. This idea goes back to 1898, when psychologist Norman Triplett discovered that a cyclist will ride faster if they are racing against another cyclist rather than just against the clock. In the world of business, rivalry can also be very motivating. The rivalry between Steve Jobs at Apple and Bill Gates at Microsoft was no secret, for example. Even in the lower echelons of workplace society, just sitting next to someone else in the office, a low-level rival, can boost people's productivity.

A report in the *Academy of Management Journal* in 2016 suggested that a 'good' rival has three key qualities: similarity, repeated competition and competitiveness. Thus, we can only be a rival of someone who is like us; we need frequent opportunities to compete against them; and there has to be something to win. There needs to be a winner and a loser. These conditions will lead us to push ourselves as hard as possible to be the winner.

Of course, there is a downside to rivalry too, usually tied to the fact that someone has to lose. While rivalry is associated with better work performance, for example, it is also associated with increased risk-taking and unethical behaviour, as people are driven to further lengths to undermine their rivals. In such cases, it is probably better to try to build bridges with the rival, as any benefits risk being outweighed by the costs.

THE DARK TRIAD OF PERSONALITY TRAITS: WHAT ARE THEY AND DO I HAVE THEM?

Within the world of personality psychology, there is a term to describe a particular cluster of negative personality traits that often occur together – the Dark Triad. Coined in 2002 by Canadian psychologists Delroy Paulhus and Kevin Williams, this term refers to the combination of narcissism, Machiavellianism and psychopathy. People who are high on the scale for all three of these personality traits are often considered to be rather toxic, though many perfectly decent people have some of these traits at lower levels.

NARCISSISM
People high on this scale are often self-important, selfish, arrogant, boastful and lacking in empathy. They are almost exclusively focused on themselves.

MACHIAVELLIANISM
This term originates from the Renaissance political philosopher Niccolo Machiavelli, and includes traits such as manipulation, self-interest, lack of emotion, absence of morality and deceit.

PSYCHOPATHY
People high on this scale display anti-social behaviour, lack of empathy or remorse, and are cold and uncaring.

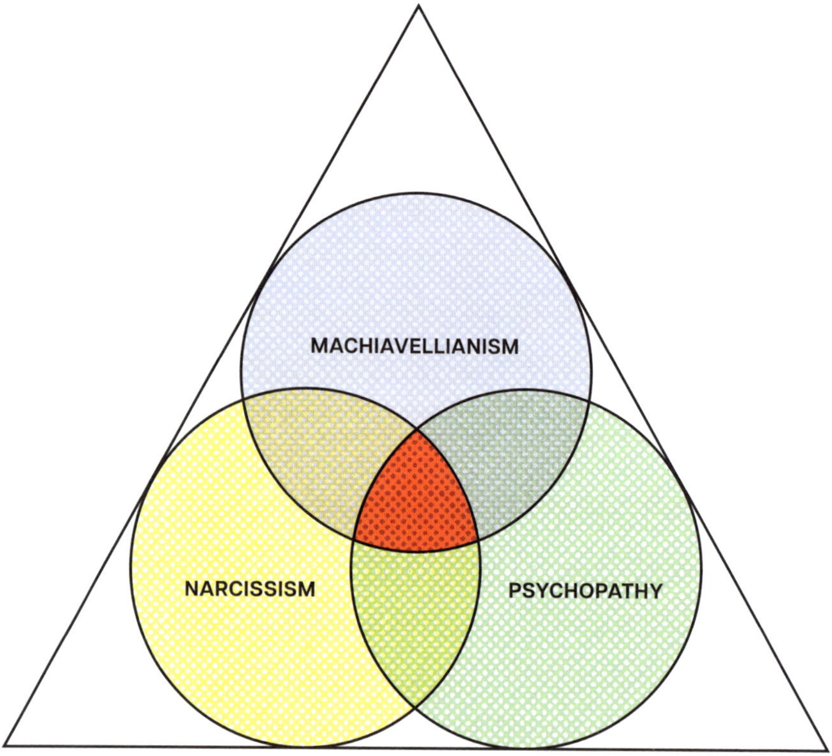

THE DARK TRIAD OF PERSONALITY

People who score highly on all three parts of the Dark Triad are unlikely to be the nicest folk in the world. While they don't have the traits strongly enough to warrant clinical classification (such as Psychotic Personality Disorder), they exhibit them enough to have a negative impact on people around them, especially in romantic relationships and in the workplace. They are often referred to as toxic.

The number or percentage of the population who have the Dark Triad is not really known, but this cluster of traits does tend to occur more in men than in women and dark personality types have been associated with racist or prejudiced attitudes.

KEEP AN EYE OUT FOR RED FLAGS

Identifying someone with the Dark Triad can be difficult, because they are masters at masking, deception and manipulation. But red flags include:

- Constantly doing things that only serve their own self-interests, using manipulation or deception to get their own way.
- Showing no concern or remorse for other people's feelings, unless it is in their interest to do so.
- Lying or using underhand tactics to get others to agree with them or to get what they want.
- A history of difficult relationships – lots of broken romantic relationships and lots of different jobs, with references to 'personality differences' at previous workplaces. They seem to leave a trail of hurt and conflict wherever they go.
- Constant shameless and boastful self-promotion while callously putting everyone else down.
- Impulsivity, especially with regards to doing things to get their own way – maybe even committing crimes if that's what it takes.

If you think you are dealing with someone with a dark personality, try to protect yourself by having clear boundaries, assuming they only ever have their own best interests at heart and not putting your trust in them. In short, keep your distance as much as you can.

WHY WE'RE DRAWN TO DRAMA (AND HOW TO AVOID IT)

Many of us love a bit of drama, even if we feel somewhat guilty about it. We rubberneck at a car accident, curtain-twitch when an ambulance appears in our street, can't look away if we see two people having a brawl and get excited over a shared piece of juicy gossip. We might even secretly enjoy being at the centre of some drama, preferring life to be full of dramatic ups and downs, rather than stable and mundane all the time.

It's probably easy to understand why drama, with all its excitement, can add some sparkle to our otherwise humdrum lives. This is what psychology has to say about why we're drawn to drama:

- **ADRENALIN AND ENDORPHINS**
  When we get caught up in the excitement or even anxiety of a drama, we produce adrenalin, which can feel exciting, and endorphins, which feel good. The feelings associated with these chemicals can be quite addictive, making us want to repeat experiences that generate them.

- **DISTRACTION**
  Drama can provide us with excellent distraction from our day-to-day concerns or mundane life. We can be otherwise preoccupied with our own worries about work, family and relationships, but as soon as we get embroiled in some drama, all that goes out of the window as we focus solely on the attention-grabbing excitement playing out around us. This gives us respite from our daily cares.

- **SENSE OF IMPORTANCE**
  Drama is all about attention and many of us love to be the centre of attention – it makes us feel important and of value. When we are involved in or are witness to some particularly juicy drama, we have first-hand knowledge and information that we can share with

others who will be desperate to hear all about it. Knowing that people are queuing up to engage with us can be quite intoxicating.

- **COUNTERS BOREDOM**
  Drama gives us something big to be involved in. This can be especially appealing to people who may feel that nothing major happens in their life or that they are stuck in a rut dealing with insignificant stuff. Being involved in or witness to a big drama changes all that; it breaks the routineness of life and allows us to get stuck into something more emotionally demanding.

- **IT IS FAMILIAR**
  Some people grow up among drama – life at home was always dramatic with full-on conflict, rows and arguments. Perhaps there were shouting matches, objects being flung, people walking out or slamming doors. Even though they might not like it, this sense of unpredictability is familiar and thus feels comfortable – leading to a craving for ongoing drama.

HOW TO CUT DOWN THE DRAMA IN YOUR LIFE

So, if drama is a big draw, can we avoid it if we want to? The first step is to acknowledge the pull that drama has on you. Work out which of the reasons listed above most motivates you in pursuit of drama. If you realize that boredom or striving for a sense of importance is your driver, look at changing those things in your life.

In general though, the following strategies may be useful in helping you resist the pull of drama:

- **MIND YOUR OWN BUSINESS!**
  Getting sucked into other people's drama may seem exciting, but it can end up causing all sorts of issues. Avoid it by asking yourself if the events unfolding affect you. If not, keep your head down and step away.

- **ESTABLISH BOUNDARIES**
  A lot of drama happens because we have weak boundaries about what is and is not acceptable. Shouting matches or hurling insults may be dramatic, but you don't have to engage. Know what your hard lines are and walk away if they are crossed.

- **DON'T STIR THE POT**
  Some of us love to feed the drama by sharing juicy gossip or adding fuel to the fire with titbits of information. If you have knowledge to share, consider whether this will fan the flames or douse them. If it is the former, consider keeping this information to yourself instead.

- **EXAMINE YOUR RELATIONSHIPS**
  If you are in a relationship that is an emotional roller-coaster, consider whether you are really benefitting from it. Sometimes all the drama is just not worth it.

THE BYSTANDER EFFECT: WHY WE ARE MORE LIKELY TO GET HELP IF THERE ARE FEWER PEOPLE AROUND

Many of us would probably prefer to walk home at night along a busy street rather than a quiet one. Surely it's safer to be in a crowd than on our own? If we needed help, surely the more people there are around, the more likely it is that someone would step up and help us?

Unfortunately, psychology tells us that this is not the case. We are, in fact, more likely to get help if there are fewer people around. The tragic case of Kitty Genovese in 1964 illustrated this phenomenon, later termed 'the Bystander Effect' by psychologists John Darley and Bibb Latané. Catherine Susan 'Kitty' Genovese was stabbed to death by Winston Moseley near her home in New York City. What was notable about this senseless murder was how many neighbours witnessed the attack, but did nothing to help her. Later investigation by police revealed that approximately a dozen individuals nearby had heard or observed portions of the attack, although two weeks after the murder, an article in *The New York Times* was published under the headline 'Thirty-Seven Who Saw Murder Didn't Call the Police'.

Several reasons were offered as to why the bystanders did not take action. Many of them felt that surely someone else would call the police, because there were so many other witnesses. This was later described as 'diffusion of responsibility' and shows that the more people there are, the less likely anyone is to help.

As part of their research, and in order to observe how people responded when they were alone or part of a larger group, Darley and Latané tried to replicate the situation

in which Kitty Genovese's neighbours found themselves. The researchers would stage an emergency situation and measure how long it took the participants to intervene (if indeed they did intervene).

For example, in 1969, Bibb Latané and Judith Rodin (another psychologist) staged an experiment around a woman who appeared to have fallen and was hurt. When people were on their own, 70 per cent of them called out or went to help the woman, but if there were other people in the room, only 40 per cent offered to help her.

In analysing their findings, the researchers noted that our actions in an emergency will depend on a five-stage process:

1. First, people actually have to notice that something is going on. We tend to be more aware of our surroundings when we are on our own, as Latané and Darley demonstrated via a study to see how quickly people would react to the presence of smoke. They took participants to a room – either alone or with a confederate – then released smoke through a vent. While 75 per cent of the participants who were on their own reported the presence of smoke, 62 per cent of the other group did not – even when there so much smoke in the room it was difficult to see (at which point the experiment was stopped).

2. Once we have noticed a problem, we then need to interpret the situation as being an emergency. According to the 'principle of social influence', we look to other people in an emergency situation to see how they are behaving. If others are not reacting, then you probably won't perceive the situation as an emergency either. This is why when fire alarms go off, so many people stay where they are rather than evacuate.

3 The next stage is to assesses the Degree of Responsibility we feel about the problem. How much we feel it is our personal responsibility to help can depend on three things: (1) whether or not we feel the person is deserving of help, (2) whether or not we feel we have the skill to help them and (3) our relationship with the victim (we are less likely to help people we don't know).

4 We then need to consider how to help – either with direct intervention (directly assisting) or detour intervention (such as reporting an issue elsewhere). Sometimes the bystander will simply not know what to do.

5 We may then take the action needed, as long as other factors don't prevent us from doing so. The main barrier might be embarrassment in front of others – 'Suppose I make a fool of myself?' Other barriers to action may be fear or not wanting to 'get involved'.

HOW PSYCHOLOGY CAN HELP WITH A PAINFUL PROCEDURE

Pain is a marvellous and clever mechanism designed to save our lives – it's a signal that something potentially damaging or dangerous is happening to us that we need to take action to avoid. But pain can also make our lives a misery, especially when its life-saving properties are not required. Our brain cannot distinguish between the pain we feel when touching something hot (which requires us to move away to avoid further injury) and pain we feel when we are having an inoculation (which requires us to keep still and suck it up). But is there anything we can do to help us feel less pain in situations like these?

Research suggests there are a range of strategies that can help us feel less pain:

- **TRY TO RELAX**
  We feel more pain when we are stressed and anxious, so trying to relax our body and mind can help reduce the pain.

- **RUBBING IT BETTER**
  Rubbing or touching a different area of the body than the one experiencing pain can confuse the nerves because it shifts attention from one part of the body to another. This is based on the so-called Gate Control Theory of Pain – a 'gate' in the spinal cord can regulate the transmission of pain signals to the brain, and stimulating other areas can close the pain gate and open a different gate. The best way to achieve this, according to research, is to stroke gently and slowly.

- **THE PRESENCE OF OTHER PEOPLE**
  Does having a friend with you help alleviate the pain? Some studies suggest it can, but a 2017 study suggested that while people report less pain when they have someone with them (this is especially true for men if they are accompanied by another man) they still experience the same amount of pain – they just report less.

- **MOOD**
  Research suggests that people with anxiety or low mood feel pain more. For example, a study in 2001 showed that negative mood leads to a stronger feeling of pain whereas positive feelings can help to alleviate the pain.

- **CONTROL**
  Having a sense of control or empowerment can help us feel less pain. This is why patient-controlled analgesia (PCA) in hospitals is so effective – within limits, patients can administer their own pain relief via a pump and thus feel more in control. One study in the 1980s found that if women in active labour are given some control over parts of the delivery process, positive effects can be seen in terms of reduced pain.

- **DISTRACTION**
  Watching something funny or entertaining can help distract us while we undergo a painful procedure, and not focusing on the pain can help us feel it less. This is why my dentist (and others) has a screen above the dental chair so patients can watch their favourite shows. A study in 2001 showed that patients who were 'hypervigilant' about pain were more likely to report more pain than patients who were less attentive to it.

- **APPRAISAL**
  How we feel about or appraise the pain can influence our perception of it. For example, if we view the pain as catastrophic, we will feel it more acutely than if we are less concerned about what the pain signifies. Thus, if we notice a pain in our shoulder and attribute it to a sporting injury, we may feel less pain there than if we worry if could be a sign of something life-threatening. Understanding and making sense of the pain can thus help with pain management.

HAPPINESS AND WELLBEING

5.

THE SURPRISING SCIENCE OF HAPPINESS (IT'S NOT WHAT YOU THINK)

Humans have been in pursuit of happiness for as long as they have existed, but our preoccupation with it nowadays is probably unprecedented. For much of the Western world, more leisure time and less focus on survival means more energy devoted to the pursuit of happiness. These days, happiness, not survival, is our goal and a huge industry has developed to help us achieve this.

But what exactly do we mean by happiness? According to researchers Richard Ryan and Edward Deci, happiness is made up of three factors: the presence of positive emotions, the absence of negative emotions and satisfaction with life. The science of happiness involves research, mainly by psychologists, into what makes us happy. The discipline is sometimes referred to as positive psychology and reveals a number of surprising findings about what makes us happy:

1. **OUR HAPPINESS IS NOT JUST DOWN TO OUR GENES**
   It is often thought that some people are just born happier, or with a sunnier personality, than others. Some people seem to take life's ups and downs in their stride and find pleasure and joy where others see only doom and gloom. But many researchers have found that the role of genetics is not as strong as we might think and that happiness is largely determined by our experiences. This is demonstrated in the 'happiness pie' model devised by Lyubomirsky, Sheldon and Schkade in 2005, which suggests that genetics only contribute half of the determinants of our happiness levels, with a further 10 per cent being determined by life circumstances. This leaves another 40 per cent that is caused by things within our own control.

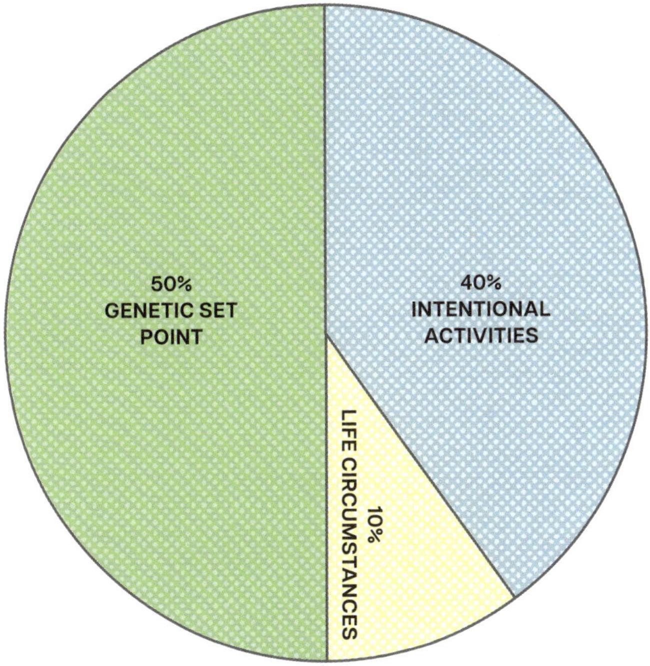

WHAT DETERMINES HAPPINESS?

2 THE BEST WAY TO IMPROVE OUR HAPPINESS IS THROUGH SOCIAL CONNECTION

How can we best use that 40 per cent in the happiness pie? Surprisingly, the answer seems to be in working on our social connections. According to Rohrer et al. in 2018, spending more time with family and friends is the best way to increase our happiness levels. And a Harvard study that started in 1938 and tracked the lives of 724 men for 75 years (making it one of the most famous longitudinal studies of all time) found that good relationships are the key factors for long-lasting happiness. Meaningful relationships make us happier than money, holidays or material possessions.

3 BEING KIND MAKES US HAPPIER

A Japanese study in 2006 showed that kind people experience more happiness and have happier memories than less-kind people. Even the thought of helping others makes us happier; brain scans have shown that just thinking about helping others activates the mesolimbic pathway in the brain, which produces the feel-good chemical dopamine. Other happiness chemicals thought to be stimulated by kindness include serotonin and oxytocin.

A 2018 review of hundreds of studies on happiness showed that performing acts of kindness boosts happiness and wellbeing. The authors found that the more acts of kindness you perform, the greater your levels of happiness will be.

4 BEING HAPPY HAS HEALTH BENEFITS

Did you know that happy people are actually healthier too? Research has shown that happiness is linked to lower heart rate and blood pressure and can even boost the immune system.

One reason that is thought to explain the link of happiness to health outcomes is that happier people tend to engage in healthier behaviours. We tend to eat healthier food when we are happy and feeling positive, may exercise more, sleep better, have more social interactions and engage in absorbing hobbies. If we are sad, depressed or unhappy, we might be more likely to engage in unhealthy behaviours such as eating junk food, being inactive and withdrawing from other people. This unhealthy lifestyle is linked to weight gain, higher cholesterol and blood pressure, and lowered immunity.

Happy people can often cope better with stresses and be more resilient. It is easier to take life's ups and downs in our stride when we feel upbeat and cheerful, compared to when we already feel brow-beaten and depressed. And, stress has a whole body of research linking it to negative health outcomes, thus reinforcing the happiness-health link. Research has even shown that happier people are less likely to undertake risky behaviours, perhaps having less need for thrill-seeking.

All of these factors explain why research has consistently shown that happier people live longer. For example, The English Longitudinal Study of Ageing published a study in 2011 that tracked over 11,000 people aged 50 and older over a nine-year period. The research found that even when taking into account factors such as age, gender, wealth, education, depression, smoking, activity levels and physical health, the risk of dying in the next five years was 35 per cent lower for the happiest group of people within the group.

5 BEING OUTDOORS CAN MAKE US HAPPIER

We are spending more and more of our time indoors – this is especially the case for children and young people. Yet research suggests that we can become happier by spending more time outdoors, especially among nature.

One study, for example, carried out by Gregory Bratman of Stanford University in 2015, assigned 60 participants to take a 50-minute walk in either an urban or in a nature setting. He measured their 'affect' (or mood) before and after the walk and found that those in the nature-walk group reported happier affect and more positive emotions than the urban walkers. Not only that, but he also used brain scanning imagery to try to figure out why the nature walkers were so much happier. He discovered increased activity in an area within the prefrontal cortex; when there is decreased activity in this part of the brain, it is associated with depression and anxiety.

CAN YOU BECOME A MORNING PERSON?

Are you an owl or a lark? Larks go to bed early and get up early, ready and alert for the day ahead. Owls, on the other hand, are grumpy if they have to get up early – they are much happier with late nights and late starts. According to one UK study back in 1998, roughly a third of us are owls and a third larks, with the rest of us not favouring either lifestyle. Our choices are not really choices, however – genetics plays a huge part in whether we are happier at the crack of dawn or at the chimes of midnight.

Popular culture tends to suggest that it is the larks who do better in life – seize the day, early bird catches the worm and all that. As Benjamin Franklin said, 'early to bed and early to rise makes a man healthy, wealthy, and wise.' There are many examples of successful early risers: Apple CEO Tim Cook has been reported to get up at 3:45am, Michelle Obama starts her day with a workout at 4.30am and Richard Branson rises at the rather more leisurely time of 5:45am.

But if you are an owl, can you make yourself into a lark? After all, most work environments favour the early riser, with the majority of workplaces and offices operating in daylight hours. The same goes for educational establishments – we can't get our kids up for school at noon. Surely it would be better for any owls among us to retrain ourselves and change our lifestyles to become morning people?

While we can't completely change our chronotype (internal clock), we can do things to influence it. If you are a wannabe lark, you could try to adjust your circadian rhythms by going to bed slightly earlier each night and setting your alarm slightly earlier in the morning. Scheduling enjoyable and fun activities earlier in the day can also encourage you to make an early start, while getting active as soon as possible after waking up can also help (although maybe not 3:45am, like Tim Cook). Getting access to natural light at the start of you day can help too, so one of those special daylight alarm clocks might be useful.

There is only so much you can do to overcome your natural inclination to owl-ness, however, so if you are really struggling to become a morning person, perhaps you should give up and embrace the later hours instead. Studies reveal that there are some advantages to being a late riser. While morning people have been shown to achieve more academically, night owls have been shown to have better memory and be more open to new experiences – they may even be more creative than morning people. Studies have shown that owls have better processing speed and cognitive ability at tasks, even when those tasks are performed in the morning. And, contrary to popular belief, owls are not unhealthier or financially poorer than larks.

Many people firmly in the owl camp can adapt their lifestyles to suit their chronotype, and in today's digital age, this has never been easier. Your most productive and happy times may be when half the population in your part of the world is asleep – but might be the time when all the larks are rising on the other side of the globe. And, with so much of our communication these days being non-synchronous (i.e. not happening at the same time), owls can fire off emails and work projects during the night ready for the larks to open up the next morning while the owls are catching up on their shut-eye. It's never been easier to be a happy owl!

THE WORLD'S HAPPIEST COUNTRIES

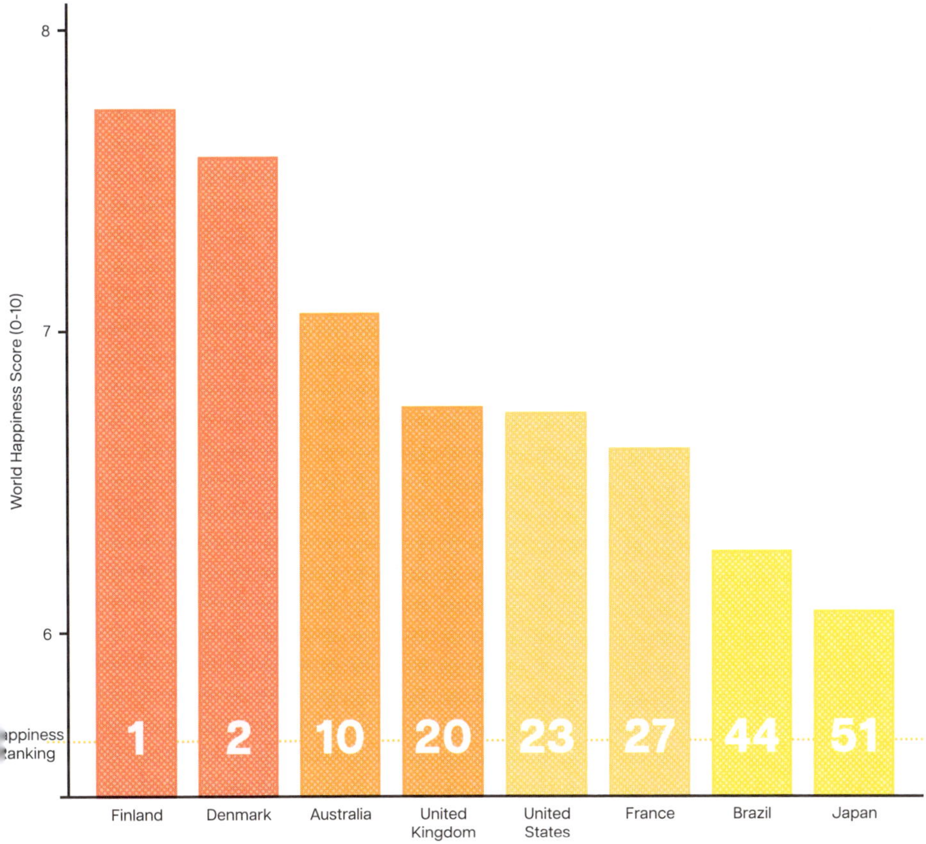

WHY HAVING MORE MONEY DOESN'T MAKE YOU HAPPIER: THE HEDONIC TREADMILL THEORY

If only we had more money, life would surely be bliss! Imagine winning the lottery...Well, it may surprise you to know that money doesn't actually make us as happy as we might think it would. Studies repeatedly show that while it is true that money can help raise our happiness levels, it only does so up to a certain point.

Without enough money to buy the things we need – food, shelter, clothing – we may feel anxious, stressed and unhappy. Having enough money for some luxuries like holidays, meals out and entertainment, for example, can certainly add to our happiness levels, as it allows us more opportunity to do things that give us pleasure. But beyond that, having even more money does not necessarily lead to more happiness.

In 2020, researchers from the Office for National Statistics and Happy Planet Index worked out that in order for the average Briton to live a happy life, they would need a gross annual income of at least £33,864. More than that increases happiness, but previous research in 2010 suggested that anything above about £65,000 does not lead to a significant increase in happiness – though that actual figure is debatable and is thought to be closer to £110,000 in 2024.

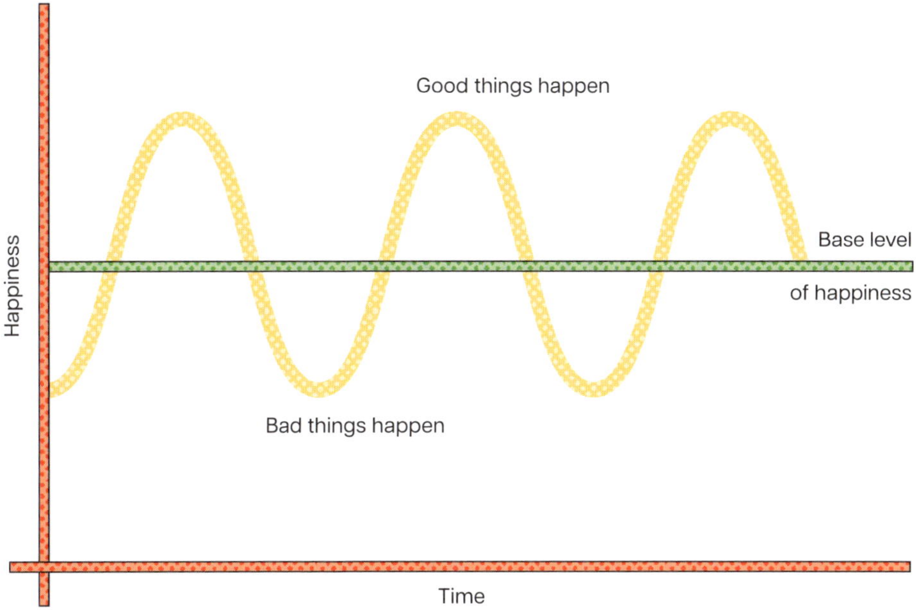

THE HEDONIC TREADMILL HYPOTHESIS

What researchers do agree on, however, is that beyond a certain threshold, our happiness does not increase incrementally in line with income. That is, if we currently earn £80,000, earning £160,000 will not make us twice as happy as we are now – though it may make us a bit happier. Below that threshold, increasing income has a much bigger impact on our happiness levels. Thus, for example, people who earn £50,000 per year are much happier than those who earn £10,000 per year, but someone on £1 million a year is not much happier than someone earning £100,000 per year. Money has less impact on your happiness the richer you get.

The reason for this is explained by the hedonic treadmill hypothesis, a psychological theory that suggests that we all have a happiness 'set point' or base level and that whatever major events happen to us, whether they be negative or positive, eventually we will return to our basic set level of happiness. This is because we adapt once the initial euphoria or low mood caused by the events passes.

For example, imagine that you move into the house of your dreams. You love the spacious rooms, the floor-to-ceiling windows and the mature gardens. Your happiness levels leap when you first move in, and you spend time just sitting and gazing at this masterpiece you now live in. After a while, however, you get used to it. You stop noticing the beautiful wallpaper and the airy kitchen. It just becomes home. Your happiness levels go back roughly to where they were before you moved in – a little higher, perhaps, due to the nicer surroundings and better facilities, but they don't stay at the same high levels as when you first moved in.

The same applies to income. That big lottery win brings all kinds of wonderful opportunities, but eventually, you will get used to the first-class travel, the five-star hotels and the designer clothes. You may even start moaning about poor service or get irritated when standards are below expectation. Happiness levels creep back down to around pre-lottery levels.

The other issue is that a lottery win, or even a promotion at work, could have an impact on your social life. Your friends may feel uncomfortable around your new wealth or resentful of your success. You start doing things that bring you into contact with wealthier people – at private members clubs, sports clubs or in business lounges at airports. Your social group changes but the wealthier set are very different from the friends you are used to. They may be 'snobbish' or entitled or have different interests than you – and being around them may not make you happy.

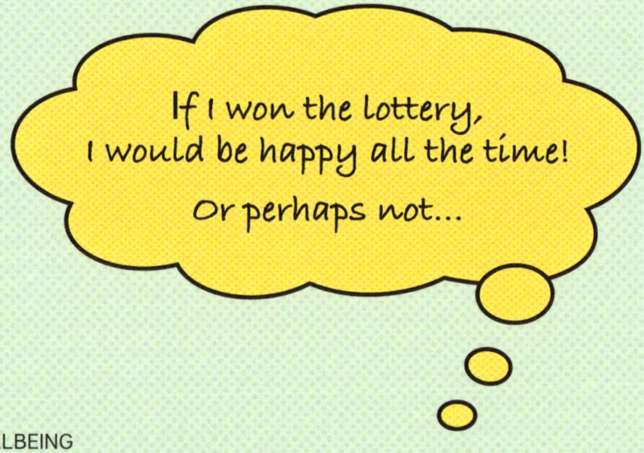

It is also human nature to compare ourselves with others. As we start moving in wealthier circles, we mix with people who are even wealthier than us – and then we feel lacking by comparison.

Of course, this is not true for everyone – there are many blissfully happy rich people! The research does not suggest that more money always makes you unhappy and, in fact, one study suggested that 80 per cent of us will be beaming with happiness as our income rises. The bottom line really is that money does not impact happiness levels as much as other factors. Happy poor people will probably be happier rich people, but if you were miserable on a lower income, you might not be significantly happier on a higher income. Other factors such as relationships and meaningfulness matter more than money.

The thing about money that really saps our happiness is yearning for more of it. A study led by Daniel Kahneman (a long-time researcher into the link between money and happiness) and Ed Diener in 2003 found that while having more money makes us happy (up to a point), seeking it does not. People who craved money were found to be less happy with their relationships, jobs and family life.

So, while we all dream of that big lottery win, getting too caught up in the fantasy of great riches will not make us happy.

RICHER OR POORER?

Would you rather earn £80,000 while all your friends earned £50,000, or £100,000 while all your friends earned £200,000?

Most people would rather earn more than their friends than less – even if, overall, that means less money. We don't want to be the 'poor' one in the crowd, always feeling inferior or envious.

HOW TO MAKE YOURSELF HAPPIER IN TEN MINUTES A DAY

If money isn't the answer, is there anything we can do to increase our happiness levels quickly? As it happens, I have created a method to do just that. It involves recording, in a journal, incidents within six key domains, for ten minutes at the end of every day. Each domain is carefully chosen and based on sound psychological theory.

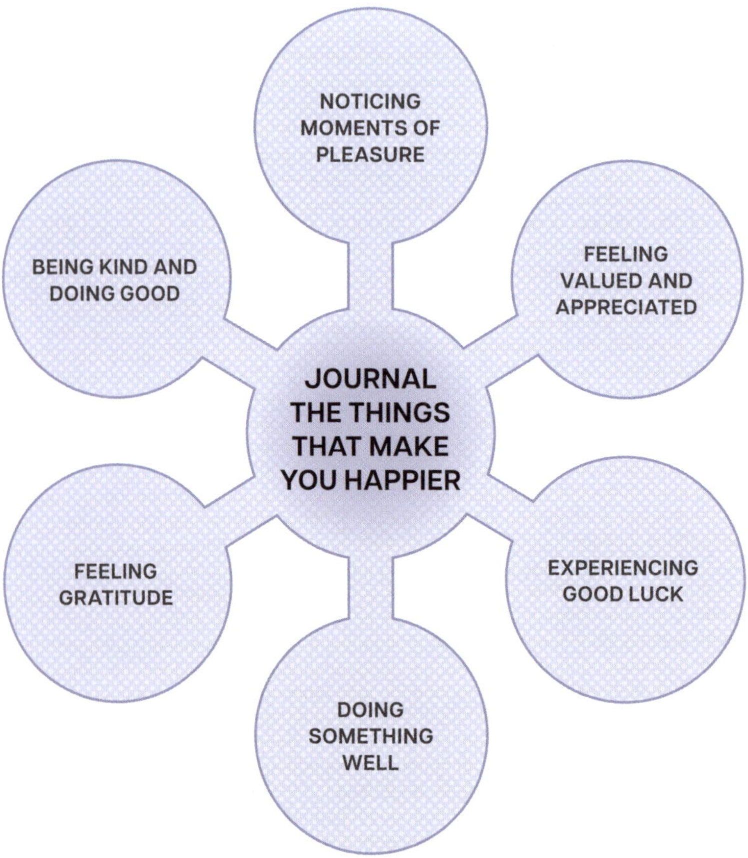

The six areas that will make you happy and that are to be recorded are:

1 **THINGS THAT WERE ENJOYED THAT DAY**
Pleasure and enjoyment are essential components of happiness, so it's vital that we do things that give us pleasure (every single day) and take notice of them. Noting them focuses our mind on pleasure, helps us appreciate the small stuff and even changes our lifestyle as we do more to incorporate fun or pleasure into our day-to-day lives.

2 **POSITIVE STROKES RECEIVED**
We all need to feel appreciated and valued by others – it makes us happy to feel we have made a difference. Getting praise or a pat on the back doesn't happen that often, but when it does, noting it in your journal will help you recognize and acknowledge the difference you are making to people – and help you feel happier.

3 **ANYTHING LUCKY THAT HAPPENED**
There is some evidence to suggest that your attitude to luck influences how happy you feel. Happier people tend to think they are luckier than unhappy people do. According to a 2019 study entitled 'Do the Happy-Go-Lucky?' by Edmund Thompson, G P Prendergast and Gerard H Dericks, viewing ourselves as lucky helps us feel more optimistic and more likely to try new things. And yet, research consistently tells us that happy people are not actually any luckier – they just believe they are. This is because they are more likely to notice when lucky things happen to them, which is why this strategy of noting and recording lucky events is so useful.

4 **ANY ACHIEVEMENTS, HOWEVER SMALL**
Happy people tend to recognize their own achievements because they have a more optimistic and positive mindset that allows them to acknowledge when they have done something well rather than just focus on their shortcomings. So, in this section, write down anything you have achieved, rather than dismissing it.

5 BLESSINGS TO BE COUNTED

There is a wealth of literature linking gratitude to happiness. The more we have to be grateful for, the more positive we feel. For example, in 2003, two psychologists, Robert Emmons of the University of California, Davis, and Michael McCullough of the University of Miami, found that people who wrote about things they were grateful for were happier than people who wrote about things that irritated them. Similarly, Martin Seligman, a well-known researcher in the field, found in 2005 that writing a letter of gratitude had more of a positive impact on happiness than any other intervention.

6 ACTS OF KINDNESS PERFORMED

Research has consistently shown that being kind to others and performing good deeds stimulates serotonin and dopamine in our brains, which makes us feel good. People who regularly perform good deeds feel that they are contributing to society and that they have a purpose in their life. A Japanese study in 2006 showed that kind people experience more happiness and have happier memories than less-kind people – and that noting acts of kindness for a week can make us happier.

TRY THIS:

GO IN SEARCH OF PLEASURE

When did you last do something you enjoyed or gave you pleasure? If you are struggling to think of something, you really need to introduce more fun and pleasure into your life. Start seeking out stuff to enjoy – a coffee with friends, a soothing bath, a walk in the sunshine, an absorbing book. Note them down at the end of the day to encourage you.

WHY TOO MUCH SELF-CARE CAN BACKFIRE

These days, we are constantly being urged to prioritize self-care and create a routine that focuses on improving our diet, exercise, skincare, thoughts, relaxation, respite, body, soul and more. The hashtag selfcare has had billions of views on TikTok and can be found in millions of Instagram posts. But while self-care is undoubtedly an important part of keeping us healthy, too much really can backfire.

The problem is that our self-care routines can take up so much time that they eat into our lives in a way that causes us stress. Mindfulness programmes, exercise regimes, healthy meal prep, constant journaling, wading through self-care books, regular massages, complicated skincare regimes, candle-lit baths, learning a language, doing Wordle, seeing friends, crafting, playing sport, taking up new hobbies...the list is exhausting, never mind the actual doing of it all. How on earth are we also expected to fit in a full working day, childcare and household chores?

We are blessed to have more leisure time than ever before, thanks to labour-saving gadgets and working-time directives, but we are also filling it more and more with self-care activities that are in danger of taking over.

So why are so many of us drowning in these self-care rituals? The problem can be that much of our self-care is driven by fear. We are bombarded with messages that threaten dire consequences if we fail to take heed – do you really want your brain cells to die because you can't be bothered to do a daily puzzle? Do you really want wrinkles because you can't find time to slather expensive serum, facial oil and moisturizer on your face twice a day? Do you really want your insides to rot due to a sluggish digestive system that could be cured with an hour of special yoga? Of course not! We don't want any of that – where do we sign up?

Then there are all the TikTok influencers, with their serene faces and taut bodies, promising that we can look and be like them if only we just invested in ourselves a bit more. And yet when we do, we don't look the same, which ends up making us feel worse than when we started.

There's a big difference between self-care we practice because we deserve to feel good, and self-care routines we adopt out of fear or because we don't feel we are enough without them. Self-care can also become toxic when we use it to distract ourselves from our day-to-day reality, to avoid responsibility or challenging emotions.

So how do we know when self-care is too much? Watch out for these warning signs:

- You are getting stressed trying to fit in all of your self-care activities – but even more stressed at the idea of leaving some of them out.

- You do not enjoy an aspect of self-care but are afraid to stop doing it.

- You can't afford all the self-care strategies you are implementing.

- You are neglecting your family and friends in favour of your self-care regime.

- You become obsessed with tracking, monitoring and recording your self-care rituals.

- You are constantly reading and researching new ideas and following influencers religiously.

The reality is that self-care will not solve all of our problems – it won't, on its own, make us happy. If we are unhappy or depressed or can't sleep, no amount of candles, seaweed wraps or raw food is going to make us better.

THE PARADOX OF CHOICE: WHY HAVING MORE OPTIONS MAKES YOU LESS HAPPY

When I was little, only three types of ice cream were available – vanilla, strawberry and chocolate. None of these options excited me and I would always turn to an ice lolly for a cold treat instead. But then, oh joy, the world changed, American-style ice cream arrived in the UK and choosing between 30 options became the norm. These days, a trip to the ice-cream parlour sees me almost paralysed with indecision – my favourite flavours now include cookies and cream, lemon meringue pie and caramel pretzel. My mouth is watering as I write this.

Choosing just one (OK, I admit, two) flavours for a treat is agonizing. Whatever I pick, I am left wondering if the rejected option might have made me happier. And that's before I get onto the cone and topping options. Having too much choice is a paradox – it is wonderful but also stressful.

This is the so-called paradox of choice, a term coined by American psychologist Barry Schwartz who postulated in 2004 that the more choice we have, the less satisfied we are with our decision. This is because the more choice we have, the more we have to think as we weigh up the options, leading to higher cognitive load. This leads to what is called 'decision fatigue' (this can be illustrated by the relief we might feel when one of our options turns out to be unavailable – phew, a decision has been made for us!) and ultimately 'buyer's remorse'. Schwartz came to the conclusion that too much choice actually limited our freedom rather than extended it, as demonstatred in an intriguing study involving gourmet jam. He found that when faced with 24 flavours, people were less likely to buy a jar of jam than when they were only six options.

Thirty different ice-cream flavours
= an overwhelming amount of options

Chocolate, vanilla or strawberry
= a much easier decision to make

OPTION PARALYSIS

Schwartz and later researchers found that being given too much choice, even over trivial things like flavours of jam, can cause people anxiety and distress. Choice is everywhere now – what clothes to buy, what clothes to wear, where to go on holiday, what to choose at the restaurant, what kind of milk to buy, how to take our coffee, which coffee shop to choose… we make dozens of decisions every day, choosing from a wide array of options. And it can be so stressful that many people are simply unable to choose – I work with many clients who struggle with everyday decisions so much that they are almost incapacitated by choice.

When we have a small number of options, it is easy to weigh up the pros and cons of each and balance them against each other. As the number of options rises, so does the mental work involved in weighing them up, holding those calculations in our head and then making comparisons. Ideally, we'd like to create a spreadsheet, but who does that at an ice-cream parlour?

Because the mental work in comparing and contrasting options is so draining, we may end up making impulsive decisions or developing low self-esteem because we are 'indecisive'. Or we avoid making a decision at all (ever stayed in because you can't decide where to go?). And if we feel we made the wrong decision (and someone else's dish at a restaurant always look better than the option we chose!) our self-esteem takes a knock and we lose confidence in our ability to get things right.

HOW MANY DECISIONS DO YOU MAKE EVERY DAY?

Researchers at Cornell University in 2011 worked out that we make over 200 decisions every single day just about food. And a poll of 2,000 adults in 2022 found they spend an estimated three hours a day deciding what to eat, what time to go to bed, what to wear and what to watch. But there is very little research that has looked into how many overall decisions we make each day, so why not do your own research and keep a note of every single decision you make, from the time you wake up to the time you go to bed?

TRY THIS:

PRACTICE MAKING DECISIONS

If you are the sort of person who finds it hard to decide, prefers others to make the decision, suffers a lot of post-decision regret or doesn't trust yourself to make the 'right' decisions, then you are probably struggling with too much choice.

You can learn to cope better with choice by practising making decisions about trivial stuff and learning to live with the consequences. With so much choice, it is inevitable that we won't always make the perfect or even the best decision, but we have to live with that rather than be beset by regret.

So, start making small decisions quickly, and accepting that it might not be the 'right' one, but being OK with that. Don't sweat the small stuff.

Once you have built up tolerance for that, move to the more important decisions. Use tables of advantages and disadvantages (assigning weightings too) and ask someone else for advice if needed. But at some point, make the best decision you can, because not making a decision will mean you will be left with the default option, which may not be in your best interests.

Learning to cope with the discomfort of 'post-decision regret' is part of becoming a better decision-maker.

CURIOUS QUIRKS AND QUESTIONS OF IDENTITY

6.

WHY ARE SOME PEOPLE MORE LIKELY TO BELIEVE CONSPIRACY THEORIES?

Conspiracy theories are explanations that put the blame for an event or events on some powerful group who do not want the 'truth' to be revealed. These explanations are proposed despite more probable theories being available.

All conspiracy theories have two key elements in common: there is some secret action or big cover-up, and there is a sinister motive behind it. Research in 2013 suggested that over half of Americans believe one of the most common conspiracy theories – that Lee Harvey Oswald did not act alone in the assassination of John F Kennedy. A global YouGov study in 2020 suggested that Britons were the least likely to believe in global conspiracies – 9 per cent believe the moon landings were faked, compared to 13 per cent in the US and around a quarter of people in countries such as Turkey, Saudi Arabia, Egypt, Mexico, Nigeria, South Africa, Brazil, Hungary, Greece and Spain.

Most conspiracy theories are so outlandish, with so much evidence against them, that it is hard to understand why anyone would believe them. Paul McCartney, for example, is alive and well at the time of writing – thousands and thousands of people have seen him in the flesh on stage since his supposed death in 1966. To believe he is dead seems bizarre. The most bizarre conspiracy theory is surely the Birds Are Not Real one, which maintains that all flying feathered creatures are, in fact, drones.

SOME OF THE MOST FAMOUS CONSPIRACY THEORIES OF ALL TIME INCLUDE:

- The moon landings were a hoax.
- The Great Pyramid of Giza was built by aliens.
- 9/11 was an inside job.
- The Holocaust did not really happen.
- Princess Diana's death was not an accident.
- The JFK assassination was a cover-up.
- Paul McCartney has been dead since 1966.
- COVID-19 was not real and the vaccinations were designed to track or harm people.
- The condensation trails behind planes in the sky are in fact 'chemtrails' – dangerous chemicals being sprayed onto the people below.

TRY THIS:

ASK YOURSELF: WHY DO I BELIEVE WHAT I BELIEVE?

- What are my fears, beliefs and values? How do they affect my decisions and how I interact with people?
- Do I have prejudices and believe in stereotypes? Why?
- Do I feel disadvantaged? In what way?
- Do I feel the need to blame somebody else? Why?
- How do I choose my sources of information?

WHAT KIND OF PEOPLE FALL FOR CONSPIRARY THEORIES?

It is often thought that people who believe conspiracy theories must have something fundamentally wrong with them, but this does not seem to be the case. According to research published in *Psychological Bulletin* in 2023, the idea that people who believe conspiracy theories are intellectually challenged or mentally unwell is not true.

The researchers examined data from a range of studies that have looked at over 158,000 participants, mainly from the United States, the United Kingdom and Poland. These studies have offered a range of reasons that make some people more vulnerable to believing these theories than others.

Belief in conspiracy theories fulfils a psychological need.

It makes people feel good to believe that they are in a small group of like-minded people who are clever enough to know the truth. It makes them feel superior to the non-believers and gives them a sense of affiliation to be part of something. Research has shown that this need is heightened if they feel rejected from other groups. Even when the believers are mocked, this just strengthens their sense of belonging and affirms their beliefs. It makes people feel safe to understand the 'real' reasons things happen, especially in a scary and chaotic world. Believing that the planes that flew into the Twin Towers in 2001 were the result of intricate government plots feels safer than believing that random terrorists around the world are using planes as weapons. Seeing clues in signs and symbols helps them feel that there is a reason for randomness, and this helps achieve a sense of safety.

Believing conspiracy theories advances a social identity for a believer.

It makes them feel that they are unique and special. They are part of a distinct minority group that they think highly of, and this gives them a sense of identity. People who are more likely to believe themselves to be special and unique are more likely to believe conspiracy theories.

People with paranoid traits, or who are highly suspicious of others, are more prone to believing conspiracy theories.

They feel that the world is dangerous, and that they must constantly be on their guard for threat, especially from institutions and governments who don't have our best interests at heart. The paranoia is not personal, like it might be with psychosis. They believe that powerful others are out to get us all, not just them. This fuels a lack of trust in those in power. According to the 2023 research, those who strongly believed in conspiracy theories were also more likely to be insecure, emotionally volatile, impulsive, withdrawn, manipulative, egocentric and eccentric.

Emotions play a role in believing conspiracy theories.

One study in 2017 revealed that when people are more anxious, they are more likely to believe in conspiracies, while an earlier study in 2016 found that stress promoted belief in conspiracies. Another study in 2009 suggested that students who were manipulated to feel out of control or powerless were more likely to believe in conspiracist ideas than those who felt more in control.

- Conspiracy theorists are more likely to believe in their intuition than in science. They trust their gut when making decisions or when deciding who to trust more than they do the evidence. They trust their instincts, which they feel have not let them down before.

- People who believe in conspiracy theories are more likely to have had unusual things happen to them that are hard to explain rationally, such as some religious experience, supernatural event or coincidence that seems incredible.

With the rise of fake news nowadays, it is getting harder to sort genuine explanations from conspiracy theories. But in order to avoid falling for a lie, it pays to ask yourself three questions: What is the evidence? What is the source for that evidence? What links the evidence to the claim? The truth is out there – if you want to find it.

HOW A JACKSON POLLOCK PAINTING RELATES TO CONSPIRACY THEORIES

Research suggests that people who see meaningful patterns in Jackson Pollock's abstract paintings are more likely to believe in conspiracy theories. Pollock was an American abstract expressionist painter whose work is described as 'unstructured' and therefore likely to feature only illusory patterns. Seeing patterns that are not there suggests making connections that don't exist, which is a central premise of the conspiracy theory. Conspiracy theorists tend to make significant connections between random events – just like they see meaningful patterns in the random shapes of a Pollock painting.

WHY YOU ALWAYS FORGET WHERE YOU LEFT YOUR KEYS (BUT NOT HOW TO RIDE A BIKE)

Surely everyone has experienced the frustration of having misplaced their car keys or house keys. When I get home, I always put my keys in the same place to avoid such panics, but every so often, it still happens! Why? And why does this always happen when I'm in a hurry?

The simple answer is that on the occasions when I lose my keys, my fail-safe system has failed me. I have not put my keys in their special receptacle (I am assuming, of course, that they haven't grown legs and walked off on their own). But why didn't I do that, and why can't I remember where I did actually put them?

There are three main reasons to account for this failure to put your keys in the usual place:

1. **DISTRACTION**
   Invariably, if I haven't put my keys in their assigned place, it is because I got distracted. It may be that my post-work hunger drove me directly to the kitchen instead of heading to the key cubby first. Or someone demanded something of me, or I received a new message on my phone. In my distracted state, the keys were slipped into my pocket, left by the toaster or possibly even placed neatly in the fridge.

2. **AUTOMATED ACTIONS**
   We handle our keys so often that we don't give them much thought and we therefore don't really notice when we put them down. As I write this, I cannot consciously recall whether I have indeed put my keys in their home or whether I have left them on my bed (a habit I have).

3. **SHORT-TERM MEMORY LIMITATIONS**
   Even if we do take note of where we put our keys ('I will leave my keys in my bag as I'm going straight out again'), this information only goes into our short-term memory, meaning it is easily lost or difficult to retrieve. By contrast, a learned skill like riding a bike is deeply embedded in our unconscious, long-term memory.

TRY THIS:

BE MINDFUL WITH YOUR KEYS

Never lose your keys again! Always put them down mindfully – notice where they are and even get in the habit of saying so out loud: 'I am putting my keys in the pocket of my winter coat.'

Having a regular spot for your keys helps too – as long as you remember to put them there...

THE DOORWAY EFFECT

It's not just keys we lose as soon as we step into our home. There is something about going into different rooms that makes us forget. We go upstairs in search of our keys and forget what we came up for or we go into the kitchen to put the kettle on but forget to make the tea.

These lapses are due to what is known as the 'doorway effect', which is when our attention is grabbed by a change in our environment. When we go through a door into a different space – a boundary between one environment and the next – our senses are assailed by different demands that weren't there in the old space: the pile of laundry we spy, the chore than needs doing, the phone call you are triggered to make. Going into a different environment is distracting – and the new images can erase the ideas we had in a previous room.

THE BIZARRE LIES WE TELL OURSELVES (AND WHY WE BELIEVE THEM)

We all do it – we lie to ourselves about all sorts of stuff and in all sorts of ways. Whether it's lies such as 'I will start back at the gym soon', 'I will just eat one biscuit' or 'I never wanted that job anyway', there are three forces at play that lead to our self-deception.

1. **COGNITIVE DISSONANCE**
   When we hold two opposing 'cognitions' (such as beliefs or facts) in our minds, we experience an uncomfortable feeling called cognitive dissonance. It is so uncomfortable that we seek to get rid of that dissonance to feel better – and sometimes we do that by lying to ourselves. For example, suppose you buy a new mobile phone. You are pretty sure you have the best possible deal for the phone you want. Two weeks later, a new model comes out that has even better features. You are now in danger of regretting your purchase and are thus experiencing cognitive dissonance – on the one hand you have bought phone A but on the other hand phone B is better. In order to reduce this dissonance and not feel uncomfortable regret, you convince yourself that phone B isn't actually any better (which is a lie) or that you don't need or want any of the upgraded features (also a lie).

2 SELF-ATTRIBUTION

Attribution is all about us trying to understand why other people have behaved in certain ways or how they have achieved certain things – we look for motives or explanations. Self-attribution is when we try to assign motives to or find explanations for our own behaviour. We lie to ourselves through self-attribution all the time. We can lie to ourselves to maintain our self-image by ascribing success to our own internal process or personality traits but attributing failures to external causes. If we are unsuccessful at a job interview, for example we could convince ourselves that the interviewer was biased or unfair (external attribution) or that we did a poor job (internal attribution).

3 THINKING BIASES

Sometimes also called cognitive distortions, thinking biases are sneaky ways in which we lie to ourselves – ways of thinking that distort reality. For example, one cognitive distortion is 'discounting the positive'. This is where we only accept negative stuff about ourselves while denying or ignoring the existence of positive stuff. So, we might average 80 per cent across all our tests, but we do badly on one paper and convince ourselves that we are failing. Another cognitive distortion is 'mental filter', which means having a particular mindset and refusing to accept anything that doesn't fit it. For example, if we believe that all young people are selfish but we come across a lovely helpful teenager, we may deny the truth, perhaps by convincing ourselves that they were a rare exception to the rule, or had an ulterior motive for being nice. This is how prejudices are formed and maintained.

WHY YOU'RE NOT THE SAME PERSON YOU WERE TEN YEARS AGO

Take a moment to think back to ten years ago. How old were you then? Did you look different? Were you doing a different job, or living in a different place? Did you have people in your life who are not around now – or vice versa? The chances are that ten years ago, life was very different for you than it is now. You may now be at a completely different stage in your career or in your private life. Your family structure, or how you spend your free time, may have changed. Your appearance and your interests may be radically different.

So many factors influence us across a span of ten years that, when added up, mean we are not the person we were then:

- **LIFE EVENTS**
  Few of us will have experienced no major life events within a ten-year timeframe. We may have met our life partner or split from them, had a baby or had a grown-up child leave home. We may have gone to university or started a new job. We may have been bereaved or moved house or even country. Each of these life events has an impact on how we view ourselves and the world. Sometimes these impacts will be negative, but they can be positive too. Life events can make us more stressed, happier, more settled or content. Or they can make us fearful or hyper alert to threat, or sensitive to criticism. They can make us work harder or make us give up.

- **NEW EXPERIENCES AND LEARNING**
  Over a ten-year period we will have learned so much. Some of that will be intentional learning – courses, training, a new language – but a lot will be unintentional – learning about different cultures while on holiday or figuring out how to get things done when faced with a barrier. All these learning experiences change us.

- **SOCIAL CHANGES**
  Some people stay within the same social groupings all their lives but many of us are more fluid in our friendships. We might have drifted away from some people but become closer to others. New people in our lives will have an impact on our outlook, values and opinions – and new people in *their* lives will even have an indirect influence on us.

- **PHYSICAL CHANGES**
  Every one of us has grown older over the past ten years! Depending on our age, physical changes could include decreased mobility, poorer eyesight (or better, if we have had cataract surgery, for example), weight loss or gain, different energy levels or chronic pain. Our hormone or neurotransmitter production may have changed too. These will all contribute to a new self.

- **WORLD CHANGES**
  The world is changing at a fast pace and these changes are inevitably going to impact our attitudes, belief systems, opinions and outlooks. New technological developments or discoveries, new ways of working or new leisure activities, new regimes and political systems – these will all influence us and change who we are.

TRY THIS:

LOOK BACK AND TAKE STOCK

On one side, list all of your life events from the past ten years. For example, a new job, a new family member or a bereavement, a new home. On the other side, write what impact these events have had on how you feel, how you think, what you believe, what your values are, what your priorities are, how you see the world or other people, how you see yourself. This will show you how you have changed over the past ten years.

Life events	Impact

WHY YOUR ACCENT CHANGES WHEN YOU'RE NERVOUS - OR AROUND CERTAIN PEOPLE

Accents and dialects form an important part of our social identity – they immediately identify our origins and where we 'belong'. While far from home, we might meet someone from the same region we are from and have an immediate connection of culture, history, geography and even values associated with that place.

In a relatively small country like the UK, there are around forty different regional accents! How did so many accents in such a small geographical area come about – and why do our own accents vary according to our emotions or who we are talking to?

Accents will originally have formed when groups of people were isolated from other groups and developed their own mannerisms. From an evolutionary perspective, it made sense to adopt the habits and styles of your clan, so that you could fit in and benefit from their protection. Anyone speaking differently could immediately be outed as 'alien' and not part of the group – and possibly a threat on the group's resources.

Accents would also have been influenced by incomers, if there were a large enough group of them (often as the result of an invasion or migration). Thus, in the UK, for example, regional accents might have developed from an influx of Danes or Saxons at one point.

The accent we grew up with can change across our lifespan, but also across the day, depending on our situation. This is largely due to a process called social facilitation theory. We are sociable animals and when we interact, we try to do things that make the wheels of social interaction run as smoothly as possible. We want to fit in and we want others to feel they belong – this helps us get along, like each other and form group bonds. One way we can do this is by subtly adapting our accent to more closely match that of the person we are talking to, or by trying to minimize the differences between our accents. So, if we move to a new region, we slowly start to adapt to the local accent and vocabulary. Even if we speak to someone with a different accent, we might subtly pick up their intonations or tone down our own. For example, people with strong regional accents may tone them down in a job interview.

So why does our accent change when we are nervous? That is because, when nerves take hold, we are less able to exert cognitive control over everything – we get distracted by whatever is making us nervous. We might want to focus our attention on the content of what we are saying or on monitoring the other person. Because we are less focused on the fine motor control of how we are speaking we are more likely to revert to more familiar patterns of speech such as our childhood dialect; these are more ingrained and require less cognitive effort. So, when we are nervous, our faded regional accent may suddenly become more pronounced!

HOW MUCH DOES YOUR NAME IMPACT YOUR IDENTITY?

Names are so fundamental to us. Yet we don't get to choose our birth names and are largely stuck with them for life. They are so much part of our identity that many of us get really irritated if they are spelled or pronounced wrongly. As personality psychologist Gordon Allport said in 1961, 'the most important anchorage to our self-identity throughout life remains our own name'. Historically, taking away our names meant stripping away our identities. Enslaved people and victims of the Holocaust were given numbers instead of names – in the case of Auschwitz victims, these numbers were even tattooed onto their arms.

US psychologist Jean Twenge conducted research in the 2000s that suggested that people who didn't like their own name tended to have poorer psychological adjustment. Their self-esteem and confidence was knocked by having a name they disliked. Many people adopt 'nicknames' that are some variation of their given name, usually a shorter derivative – Alex, Jamie, Matt, Sue, Gill, Steph, Steve, Pat, Mo...

Some people so hate the identity they feel their given name bestows on them that they change it completely. Many choose a name that better matches their gender identity, for example, while others adopt a name that reflects their religious or cultural identity.

But how do names assume an identity? To answer this, we have to go back to birth and consider how a parent decides what to call their precious offspring. Names may reflect current trends, or the choice may be inspired by a celebrity or someone they admire. Sometimes names are chosen for their meaning or to reflect the time of year at which the child was born. Many parents now want to give their child a 'unique' name that will make them stand out from the crowd.

All this means that a desired identity is forced on us at birth. We are expected to live a life that matches our ascribed identity, with certain names associated with certain stereotypes or cultural expectations. Research has shown that people with religious-sounding names can experience prejudice and this can impact their self-identity, sometimes making them identify more strongly with their religious group. A German study found that having an unfashionable name can lead to more rejection on dating sites than having a trendy name. Other studies have suggested that we might even be less likely to help someone with a less appealing name. Such social rejection shapes our sense of identity: we might become distrusting and resentful, or start leaning towards certain groups or interests that are more accepting. According to one study at the Institute of Psychology in Beijing, we might even be more likely to become criminals.

NAMING BABIES IS EASIER IN SOME COUNTRIES THAN OTHERS

In Denmark, parents have to choose their baby's name from a government-approved list of 7,000 possibilities. Icelandic parents get an even shorter list of options: 1,800 girls' names and 1,700 boys' names.

Below, and on the following pages, are some common types of names along with the impact they might have on our identity:

UNIQUE NAMES

Does having a unique name bestow advantages to a developing identity, as modern parents seem to hope for? It could do – the Beijing study found that a unique name was more associated with an unusual career choice, such as being a film director or a judge. It would seem that someone with a unique moniker internalizes that sense of specialness and does, on average, live up to that identity.

Other research suggests that unique names help us become more creative. Because our self-identity develops with us believing ourselves to be different from our peers, we start to look for more creative or unusual solutions to problems.

On the other hand (there's always another hand in psychology!) earlier studies found that men with uncommon first names were more likely to drop out of school and be lonely later in life. One study found that psychiatric patients with more unusual names tended to be more disturbed. However, this early research should perhaps be taken with a pinch of the proverbial salt, since these days, having an unusual name is so much more common and accepted.

NAMES THAT MATCH CAREERS

There are a surprising number of people with names that perfectly match their career choices, which is known as an aptronym. These are usually surnames, but are still good illustrations of the impact that names can have on our identity. Of course, originally many of our surnames would have, been based on our profession (Smith, Taylor and Baker, for example) but nowadays it is the other way around. 'Nominative determinism' – the idea that the meaning of our names influences our life decisions, explains why there are a surprising number of neurosurgeons called Dr Brain in the English-speaking world. The idea behind nominative determinism is that we unconsciously prefer things that we associate with ourselves.

NAMES WITH MEANING

Does Grace grow up to be graceful? Will Leo become strong as a lion? Giving a child a name loaded with meaning can put pressure on them to live up to expectations.

FAMOUS NAME CHANGES: WHO BECAME WHO?

REGINALD DWIGHT	MARILYN MONROE
STEFANI GERMANOTTA	CHAPPELL ROAN
ISSUR DANIELOVITCH	BRUNO MARS
PETER GENE HERNANDEZ	LADY GAGA
CARYN ELAINE JOHNSON	VIN DIESEL
NORMA JEAN BAKER	ELTON JOHN
MARK SINCLAIR	JAMIE FOXX
ERIC MARLON BISHOP	KIRK DOUGLAS
KAYLEIGH ROSE AMSTUTZ	WHOOPI GOLDBERG

NAMES TRADITIONALLY ASSOCIATED WITH THE OPPOSITE GENDER

Marion Morrison became an icon of Hollywood's Golden Age, starring in dozens of Westerns and war films despite (or maybe because of) his traditionally female first name. You might know him better by his professional name, John Wayne. Psychologist David Figlio of Northwestern University in Illinois found that boys given traditionally female names tended to be more unruly and have discipline issues. The study also found that girls given traditionally feminine names were far less likely to pursue maths after the age of 16 than girls given names seen as predominantly male. A US study of 1,000 pairs of female twins who were given names at either end of the naming spectrum found that 'Alex' was twice as likely as her sister 'Isabella' to take maths or science at a higher level.

TRADITIONAL NAMES

What is the impact of growing up being one of four Hannahs in your class or three Mohammads at work? Research suggests that people with names that are familiar and easy to pronounce are seen as more trustworthy and likeable. Of course, what is familiar and easy to pronounce depends very much on the culture you live in. But having a more common name may also mean having to work harder to forge a unique identity – your name may be widely shared, so you may seek to set yourself apart in other ways. This can impact your life choices and personality. However, giving a child a name that is closely associated with a particular religious or minority cultural identity can also lead to them experiencing a closer bond with their community and their heritage.

WHO BECAME WHO: Reginald Dwight became Elton John, Stefani Germanotta became Lady Gaga, Issur Danielovitch became Kirk Douglas, Peter Gene Hernandez became Bruno Mars, Caryn Elaine Johnson became Whoopi Goldberg, Norma Jean Baker became Marilyn Monroe, Mark Sinclair became Vin Diesel, Eric Marlon Bishop became Jamie Foxx, Kayleigh Rose Amstutz became Chapell Roan.

IT'S ON THE TIP OF MY TONGUE! BUT WHY?

The tip-of-the-tongue (TOT) phenomenon, or lethologica, is something we all experience – that frustrating feeling when the word we are thinking of feels like it is just out of reach. We know that we know it, but we just can't quite bring it to mind. We may even feel that we know what letter the word begins with, although it can turn out we're wrong about that. I was once trying to recall the name of a place where I had stayed in the Lake District in northern England – all I could recollect was that it began with the letter 'S'. It turned out to be Eskdale, so I was kind of right.

According to a 2014 study, that 'It's on the tip of the tongue!' feeling is universal – it is thought to be experienced all over the world, by all cultures, in all languages. A study in 2020 suggested that we tend to have this experience about once a week, but this can increase to daily as we get older. It might be that as we are building more memories and knowledge over time, we are thus are more likely to experience TOT. However, it may just be that we notice these things more as we get older because we worry about them more.

The most commonly experienced TOT words tend to be proper nouns like the name of a person or a place. TOT words are different, however, from other things we can't remember. In the TOT state, we feel we know the word but are struggling to fully access it. The solution is often to stop trying to recall it and the issue then often spontaneously resolves itself in a way that true loss of memory doesn't.

It is not fully known why or how this phenomenon happens, but a number of theories have been put forward. One is the so-called 'direct access' view, which suggests that we have enough memory to know the word is there in our memory, but that something is blocking us from reaching it. The blockers may be related or similar words that interfere with the retrieval process. The reason that stopping trying to recall the word we are searching for often works is because it causes the blocking words to be forgotten, thus allowing access to the correct word in our memory.

WHY DO PEOPLE SEE ELVIS IN CLOUDS?

Have you ever seen a cloud that looks like a face? Or perhaps you've spotted a face in a rock formation or an electrical outlet or some other inanimate object? This phenomenon of seeing faces in random places is called pareidolia – and it also explains why there are so many reported sightings of 'ghosts'.

This psychological effect is not new. Descriptions of pareidolia are found in Leonardo da Vinci's 16th-century *A Treatise on Painting*, in which he writes that 'by throwing a sponge impregnated with various colours against a wall, it leaves some spots upon it…a variety of compositions may be seen in such spots, according to the disposition of the mind …such as heads of men…'

Pareidolia was first researched scientifically in the late 1800s, when a German psychologist by the name of Gustav Fechner discussed the human inclination to see faces in inanimate objects. The word pareidolia comes from the Greek words *pará*, meaning beside or alongside, and *eidolon*, meaning form, shape or apparition. It refers to the way the brain makes sense of random patterns by trying to impose familiar concepts onto them. In our evolutionary past, it was particularly important for us to be able to quickly identify if there was a person or animal hiding nearby who might be trying to harm us. We thus needed a way of quickly deciding if a pattern or image was likely to be animate or not, and it was in our best interests to prefer 'false positives' to false negatives. In other words, it was safer for us to see faces that were not there (and run away) than to miss faces that were there (and remain in place and be attacked).

The oldest and most common example of pareidolia is perhaps the face of the man in the moon. Images of Jesus are also commonly found in random places. To date, Jesus has been spotted in a frying pan, a pizza, a coffee cup, a tortilla and a slice of toast. In 2002, twenty thousand pilgrims travelled to Bangalore to pay homage to a chapatti with the image of Jesus burned into it. Mother Teresa was famously found in a cinnamon bun in Nashville and a kettle thought to resemble Hitler was identified (and, worryingly, snapped up by enthusiasts) in American department store JC Penney in 2013. And, of course, there's the King of Rock 'n' Roll. Elvis may be dead, but his image apparently lives on in a potato crisp, a tree trunk and the bottom of an almost empty pot of tomato ketchup from a fast-food restaurant. Kate Middleton, now the Princess of Wales, was reportedly 'seen' in a jellybean in 2011 (mango-flavoured, if you are interested). One believer even made a fortune from discovering the face of the Virgin Mary in her grilled cheese sandwich, reportedly selling the sandwich for $28,000 on eBay in 2004. A chicken nugget depicting George Washington only managed to net its finder $8,000 in 2012.

HOW DOES PAREIDOLIA HAPPEN?

Seeing faces in random objects – yes, even in jellybeans – is perfectly normal. Face pareidolia is not caused by any brain abnormality (as some have previously thought) but by the hard work our brain undertakes to make sense of ambiguous images. The frontal cortex in the brain detects the image and sends signals to the posterior visual cortex, which then enhances the recognizable elements in an image to try to interpret and make sense of a stimulus. Our expectations and culture play a role in this interpretation, so this is why sightings of the faces of Jesus, the Virgin Mary or Elvis are so common in certain cultures. Within Muslim cultures, for example, the name of Allah written in Arabic has been reported in a range of places too.

It isn't just faces that we find in the noise of various patterns – there are also many examples of objects, maps or animals being spotted. Some people think that the entire Loch Ness Monster phenomenon is actually a case of mass pareidolia. And of course, many reported ghost sightings are likely to have been pareidolic. Richard Wiseman, a professor of the public understanding of psychology in the UK, has a huge collection of such ghostly photos that were sent to him by members of the public.

Of course, a lot of the phenomenon of seeing faces is about wishful thinking and expectations. Ghosts or religious images can be reassuring and provide believers with evidence of their faith. When Queen Elizabeth II died in 2022, some people who 'spotted' her image in the clouds were happy to believe that this was a sign that all was well with their beloved late monarch's new existence in heaven. I'm not sure they would have felt the same reassurance from seeing her in a jellybean, but who knows?

PAREIDOLIA IN UTERO

It is not just to detect enemies that humans benefit from making faces out of random patterns. As social creatures, we are biologically hard-wired to seek out faces from a very early age – even while still in the womb (where we can't possibly have encountered an actual face yet, unless we are a twin). A study in 2017 using 4D technology found that unborn babies will show a preference for face-like stimuli over scrambled or upside-down configurations, even if this face-like shape is very basic – just two eyes and a mouth. Certainly new-born babies have been shown to demonstrate a preference for face-like patterns, and babies as young as ten months old will show signs of pareidolia – suggesting that we really are primed to detect faces everywhere, with only the slightest of hints.

THE MANDELA EFFECT: WHAT IT IS AND WHY IT HAPPENS

The Mandela Effect refers to a collective false memory. It happens when large swathes of the population remember the details of an event, situation or person wrongly. Something may be commonly believed to have occurred when it didn't, or it occurred very differently from the mass perception.

The term originated in 2009, when paranormal researcher Fiona Broome discovered that she, along with many others, believed that Nelson Mandela had died in prison in the 1980s, when he actually did not die until 2013, and was released from prison in 1990. She was shocked to find that many people remembered details of Mandela's death that had not happened, such as his funeral or a speech given by his widow. Or perhaps you recall the iconic image of the 'Tank Man', the protestor who stood in the path of a line of approaching tanks in Tiananmen Square in 1989? Contrary to common collective memory, he was not run over and killed – in fact, he is believed to have been unharmed.

So, why does the Mandela Effect happen? Like most false memories, recalled events are often influenced by expectation. We remember things as we expect them to be more than as they actually are. For example, if asked to conjure up an image of the old man in the Monopoly board game, many people (58 per cent according to one poll) describe him as having a monocle along with his top hat and cane. He doesn't – but we might expect him to, as that fits the image we might have of old-fashioned, wealthy men.

Other explanations include 'confabulation'. This is where our brain simply fills in the gaps of missing bits of memories by creating something that makes sense in context.

In the age of the internet, where information spreads rapidly around the globe, we are seeing many more instances of the Mandela Effect created by fake news. Even if this 'news' is later debunked, collective memory may cling to the old fake information, especially if it suits the narrative or is more memorable than the reality. Remember the image of Pope Francis wearing a white puffer jacket from 2023? That was as image so striking that it is more likely to be recalled than the fact that it was faked.

Famous faked images that people claim to 'remember' include President Barack Obama shaking hands with Mahmoud Ahmadinejad, the former president of Iran. Almost half of respondents in a 2010 study recalled either seeing the photograph or the actual event, even though it never happened. Or President Bush on vacation with baseball player Roger Clemens during the Hurricane Katrina disaster (again, this never happened, although around half of respondents 'remembered' it). This 2010 study found that people are more likely to 'remember' a faked event when it fits their political view or world perspective.

THE CONFORMITY EXPERIMENTS: HOW CROWDS CHANGE US

You probably like to think of yourself as an independent thinker with a mind of your own, someone who is not easily swayed by others. You can stand up for what you believe in and do the right thing, even if others are against you. This is a commendable ideal, but not even the strongest among us should underestimate the power of the crowd. Quite simply, crowds change our attitudes and our behaviours in ways we might not immediately realize.

All groups and societies have their social norms that govern the range of acceptable behaviours within that group and if we wish to fit in and be accepted, we will obey these rules. This is the concept of conformity.

The pull to conform is immense, as illustrated by some classic studies, including a study of the so-called 'autokinetic effect' carried out by Turkish-American social psychologist Muzafer Sherif in the 1930s. The autokinetic effect is a visual illusion: a single stationary source of light projected onto a screen in an otherwise pitch-dark room will appear to move. Sherif asked participants to estimate the amount by which the dot of light moved and found that when asked individually, their estimates varied, but when asked in groups of three, their estimates tended to converge around an average distance. They began to conform to the group norms.

This work was later extended into the now classic Asch paradigm. In 1956, American psychologist Solomon Asch put groups of people together in an experimental situation in which all the members of the group were confederates – except one. The non-confederate did not know that they were the only true participant in the study.

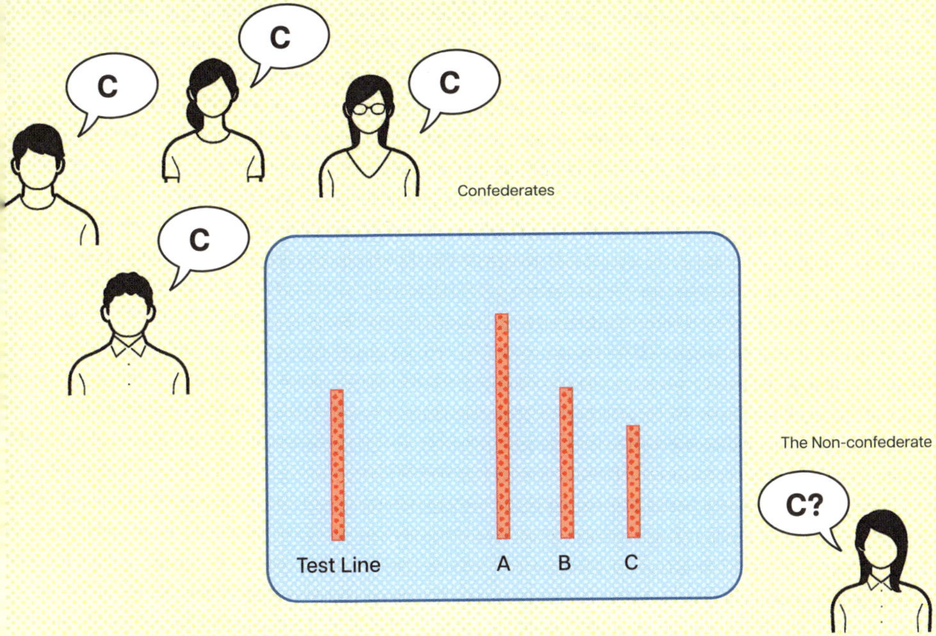

THE ASCH PARADIGM

The members of the group were all presented with a single vertical line set alongside three other lines of varying heights. The task was simple: to announce, out loud, which of the set of three lines most closely matched the length of the single line. This was an easy task and at first, the confederates gave the correct answer, as did the true participant. But after a while, things got more interesting, as the confederates would give the wrong answer. This answer was unambiguously incorrect, but guess what? The single true participant (who always had to give their answer after the confederates) went along with the stooges 75 per cent of the time.

The conformity effect could be diluted by having an 'ally' – one person in the group who gave the correct answer. The more allies they had, the less the subject of the experiment conformed. Later studies also showed that people conformed more if they liked the other group members or felt more similar to them. This shows how strong the power of conformity is and how we will deny the evidence of our own eyes in order to conform with the rest of the group.

INDEX

ABOUT THE AUTHOR

DR SANDI MANN has been a Senior Lecturer of Psychology at the University of Central Lancashire since 1998 and is an expert in emotions, especially in the workplace. She is a Director of The MindTraining Clinic (which specializes in treatment of phobias, panic attacks and anxiety conditions) and Advantage Psychology (which specializes in business-to-business training). She is a regular contributor to various media outlets as an expert psychologist, including radio, television and print media, and writes regularly for several magazines and journals, including the Huffington Post. She is also a successful author of several books on psychology.